POCKET

WARSAW

TOP SIGHTS · LOCAL EXPERIENCES

D0775517

SIMON RICHMOND

Contents

Plan Your Trip   4

St John's Cathedral (p47)
CHRISPICTURES/SHUTTERSTOCK ©

Welcome to Warsaw

Poland's capital impresses with its resilience, respect for history, diverse architecture, contemporary style and sheer *joie de vivre*. Blessed with beautiful palaces and parklands, excellent museums and a superb dining scene, this is a city that knows how to have fun, whether it be glamming up for the opera or clubbing it through the night.

Old Town Square (p46)
YIOTA FOTOU/500PX/GETTY IMAGES ©

Top Sights

POLIN Museum of the History of Polish Jews

One thousand years of Polish Jewish history. **p86**

M.STAROWIEYSKA, D.GOLIK/POLIN MUSEUM OF THE HISTORY OF POLISH JEWS © ARCHITECT: RAINER MAHLAMAKI

Warsaw Rising Museum

Understand Warsaw's heroic WWII battle. **p84**

Royal Castle

Spectacular reconstruction of the king's palace. **p36**

Museum of Warsaw

Warsaw's history imaginatively interpreted. **p40**

Palace of Culture & Science

Iconic architecture, contemporary playground. **p60**

Fryderyk Chopin Museum

World-beating collection of Chopin memorabilia. **p58**

Neon Museum

Dazzling electro-graphic art. **p122**

Wilanów Palace & Park

Superb royal country estate. **p138**

National Museum

Prime Polish art and design collection. **p106**

Łazienki Park

Gorgeous gardens, beautiful palace. **p102**

FAR RIGHT: ERIC JAMES/ALAMY STOCK PHOTO ©; RIGHT: MARCIN KRZYŻAK/SHUTTERSTOCK ©

KAV DADA/JFA/GETTY IMAGES ©

Eating

Warsaw's best chefs use top-quality produce to create dishes that please their customers and earn Michelin stars. The city's food scene is a democratic one embracing hipster food halls, revamped milk bars (self-serve canteens), and a superb selection of vegetarian and even vegan eateries.

Cooking Tours & Classes

Several companies, including **Delicious Poland** (☏791 782 792; www.deliciouspoland. com; per person 250zł) and **Eat Polska** (☏661 368 758; www. eatpolska.com; tours 290zł), offer food and/ or drinking tours of Warsaw. These usually entail visits to a handful of places with tastings paired with beer, wine or vodka.

Cooking classes are also available from Menora Info Punkt (p70) and Polish Your Cooking (p95).

Milk Bars

Warsaw's milk bars (*bar mleczny*) – dirt-cheap, self-service canteens from communist times – serve hearty Polish food, mainly vegetarian or dairy-based, hence the name. Though their ranks have thinned since their glory days, there are several popular survivors across the city, some of which have given their proletarian decor a contemporary makeover.

Useful Websites

Warsaw Foodie (https://warsawfoodie. pl) Lists new openings and plenty of options according to location and type of cuisine.

Warsaw Insider (www. warsawinsider.pl) Runs an annual Best of Warsaw selection of restaurants.

Restaurant Week (https:// restaurantweek.pl) In April Warsaw's top restaurants take part in this country-wide event.

Best Polish

Bez Gwiazdek Chef Robert Trzópek takes inspiration from across Poland for his superb, monthly changing menus. (p73)

ELEPHOTOS/SHUTTERSTOCK ©

Zoni Contemporary takes on old Polish dishes in the dramatic setting of a revamped vodka factory. (p132)

Elixir by Dom Wódki Pair beautifully presented classic Polish dishes with local vodka, honey mead or liqueur. (p73)

Dawne Smaki All the Polish staples created faithfully in a traditional setting. (p73)

Best Contemporary Cuisine

Alewino Creative dishes using seasonal produce, excellent local wines and a relaxed atmosphere. (p114)

Bibenda Crowd-pleasing, modern Polish cooking, with plenty of excellent vegetarian options. (p113)

Best Breakfast

Cafe Bristol The hearty breakfasts at this elegant cafe will set you up for the day. (p73)

Charlotte Menora Excellent bakery cafe with a Jewish flavour to its menu. (p71)

SAM Powiśle Slick and very popular bakery, deli and cafe showcasing organic produce from local suppliers. (p73)

Best Milk Bars

Prasowy This designer-updated milk bar is a hit with the students from the nearby Polytechnic. (p112)

Bar Mleczny Pod Barbakanem A New Town staple, the faded exterior only adds to its appeal. (p49)

Price Ranges

The cost of an average main course:

€ less than 30zł
€€ 30zł–60zł
€€€ more than 60zł

Drinking & Nightlife

STEVEN MAY/ALAMY STOCK PHOTO©

Varsovians are happy to go out drinking any night of the week, although you'll find more clubbing options on Friday and Saturday nights. There's little to distinguish between places that serve coffee and tea and those that serve alcohol – most do both and it really depends on the time of day you drop by.

Where to Go

Old Town & New Town
Many touristy joints, but an undeniably atmospheric spot to enjoy al fresco drinking at cafe-bars in the warmer months.

Powiśle & Northern Śródmieście For clubbing check out ul Mazowiecka, for general boozing try the shot bars in courtyards off ul Nowy Świat. Plenty of summer drinking places along the Vistula riverbank, too.

Praga & Eastern Warsaw Don't miss bar hopping along ul Ząbkowska and checking out the options at the Koneser development.

Łazienki Park & Southern Śródmieście Liberally scattered with slick cocktail bars. Also don't miss more studenty hang-outs around Plac Zbawiciela.

Vodka

Vodka is traditionally drunk from a 50mL shot glass called a *kieliszek* and downed in a single gulp. A small snack (often a pickle or piece of pickled herring) or a sip of mineral water is consumed just after drinking. Glasses are immediately refilled for the next drink and it goes quickly till the bottle is empty.

Beer

There are many brands of locally brewed *piwo* (beer) including Żywiec, Tyskie, Okocim and Lech. Beer is readily available virtually everywhere and is commonly lager, although you will find that the major brewers do also make very good porters. Polish craft brewing has really taken off and there are now well over a 1000 different local *piwo rzemieślnicze* (craft beers) to sample.

KPŽFOTO/ALAMY STOCK PHOTO ©

Best Bars

Gram Play pinball or board games at this cute, circus-themed bar in the MDM district. (p115)

PiwPaw Beer Heaven Over 80 craft ales on tap and plenty more in bottles. (p74)

Plan B An enduringly popular bar with the action often spilling out onto Plac Zbawiciela (p115)

W Oparach Absurdu Old carpets and eclectic bric-a-brac give character to this popular Praga bar. (p132)

Cosmo Cocktails that reflect the flavours of the season in a darkly sophisticated setting. (p75)

Best Cafes

E Wedel No trip to Warsaw is complete until you've sipped hot chocolate in this venerable cocoa-bean emporium. (p74)

Między Nami A 2019 makeover has breathed new life into this well-loved centrally located cafe-bar. (p75)

Stor This convivial third-wave coffee champion also has appealing bakes and snacks. (p75)

Cafe Kulturalna Trendy, sophisticated but welcoming cafe-bar in a wing of the Palace of Culture & Science. (p61)

Best Clubs

BarStudio Superior late-night dance and drinking spot inside a wing of the Palace of Culture & Science. (p74)

Klub SPATiF Dance to live music or groove along to DJs at this sophisticated and legendarily artsy club. (p114)

Smolna Hyper cool techno and electronic music club occupying an old central Warsaw building. (p76)

hopping

Warsaw has all the international brand names and malls you'd expect plus plenty of local labels and shops. The fine art of craftsmanship is well represented with several tiny ateliers in the heart of the city making a diverse range of items such as household brushes, brass light fittings, soft felt hats and fitted leather gloves.

Where to Shop

Old Town & New Town Craft sellers and jewellers hawking the local speciality amber line the cobblestone streets.

Powiśle & Northern Śródmieście Streets ul Nowy Świat and ul Chmielna are lined with boutiques; also try the giant shopping mall Złote Tarasy.

Praga & Eastern Warsaw Great for antique and vintage shopping, art galleries and contemporary Polish design at Koneser complex.

Łazienki Park & Southern Śródmieście A tale of two cities: sleek high-end boutiques along ul Mokotowska, pre-loved fashion around the Polytechnic.

Bolesławiec Pottery

Look out for shops stocking the distinctive ceramics decorated with an indigo pattern on a white background (pictured), that come from in and around the Silesian town of Bolesławiec. The region is rich in natural clay deposits and pottery has been made here since at least the 14th century. A professional ceramics school was founded in Bolesławiec in 1897 and today there are more than 20 companies in the area making hand-crafted and hand-decorated tableware and decorative objects.

Poster Art

Other wonderful souvenirs are Poland's modern and contemporary posters. Graphic poster art came to the fore in the 1950s, building on a tradition dating back to the turn of the last century. One of the most influential artists was Tadeusz Trepkowski (1914–54), who produced his best posters after WWII. His works, and those by other

LINDASKY76/SHUTTERSTOCK ©

more contemporary poster artists such as Ryszard Kaja (1962–2019) can be seen at the Poster Museum (p140), and various commercial galleries around Warsaw.

Best Local Crafts

Porcelanowa Must-have ceramics crafted by some of Poland's top potters and artists. (p80)

DecoDialogue Gorgeous Polish craftsmanship in the shape of homewares, furniture and other decorative objects. (p79)

Tcbc Gingerbread moulded into lovely decorative objects, too pretty to eat. (p117)

Best Posters & Art

Galeria Plakatu Polskiego w BUW, Warszawa Browse the striking originals and reprints of classic Polish posters. (p68)

Polish Poster Gallery If you can't see the poster in stock, check its touchscreen computerised inventory. (p53)

Galeria Art Top-quality works by members of the Association of Polish Artists and Designers. (p80)

Best Fashion

TFH Concept Streetwear as envisioned by young Polish designers at this contemporary boutique. (p81)

Acephala Showcase for Monika Kędziora's female-empowered fashions and accessories by other local brands. (p79)

Cloudmine Promoting clothes, accessories and design goods by Polish designers and artists. (p137)

Architecture

Warsaw architectural styles run the gamut from medieval churches to contemporary glass towers punctuating the skyline. Many of the city's most historic buildings, including royal palaces and nearly all parts of the Old and New Towns, are restorations or total recreations, but no less impressive for that.

PEGAZ/SHUTTERSTOCK ©

Palaces & Neoclassical

Grand palace building took off in Warsaw in the 17th century. The Dutch-born architect Tylman van Gameren (1632–1706), regarded as a master of Polish baroque architecture, worked on the Krasiński Palace as well as the original bathhouse that provided the basis for the Palace on the Isle in Łazienki Park.

In the late 18th and early 19th century, neoclassical architecture found favour in Warsaw. St Anne's Church had undergone many architectural revamps since first being built in 1454, before finally settling on its neoclassical facade in 1788. Royal architect Domenico Merlini remodelled the Palace on the Island along neoclassical lines between 1764 and 1795.

Fellow Italian architect Antonio Corazzi was responsible for a couple more neoclassical stunners: Teatr Wielki, the grand opera house inaugurated in 1833; and the Palace of the Ministry of Revenues and Treasury (1825) on Bank Sq, a building that currently serves as Warsaw's City Hall.

Art Nouveau & Art Deco

As the 20th century rolled around, art nouveau and art deco styles came into vogue. Survivors of these times include the beautifully restored market hall, Hale Mirowskie, completed in 1901 and the building that's home to the Archeology of Photography Foundation (p93).

The residential areas of Saska Kępa and Żoliborz are both treasure troves of

QUERBEET/GETTY IMAGES ©

early-20th-century architecture because they were spared the wholesale destruction suffered in central parts of Warsaw during WWII.

Contemporary Buildings

Newly constructed and creatively designed towers, such as Daniel Libeskind's Złota 44 (at 192m Europe's tallest residential skyscraper) have begun to break up the monotony of Warsaw's skyline. The Palace of Culture & Science may still be the city's tallest build-

ing, but will be toppled off its high-rise perch when the 53-storey, 320m Varso Tower, designed by Foster + Partners, tops out in 2020.

Best Historic Buildings

Royal Castle Poland's one-time royal residence has been rebuilt and restored to its former glory. (p36)

Old Town Square Admire the painstaking postwar reconstruction of the buildings that include Renaissance, baroque, Gothic and neoclassical elements. (p46)

Wilanów Palace This resplendent palace delight survived both world wars

and continues to impress with its mix of architectural styles. (pictured left; p138)

Best 20th- & 21st-Century Buildings

Palace of Culture & Science Take an architectural tour of Stalin's 'gift' to the Polish people to discover its inner beauty. (p60)

Plac Konstytucji Focal point of the Marszałkowska Residential District (MDM) where giant stone reliefs of heroic workers still look down on Varsovians. (p110)

Warsaw University Library This stunning copper-clad building was awarded top prize by the Association of Polish Architects in 2000. (p67)

Historic Sites

WITOLD SKRYPCZAK/ALAMY STOCK PHOTO ©

*Warsaw's history has been tumultu-
ous, tipping from royal grandeur to
devastating catastrophe by regular
turns. In the 20th century alone
Poland's capital flourished, was all but
destroyed during WWII, then brutally
refashioned under communist rule.
Today it is again a dynamic city reflect-
ing a thriving nation.*

WWII Impact

To fully appreciate the
city today you need
to know how it almost
was obliterated from
the map during WWII.
German bombs began
to fall on 1 September
1939 and a week later
the city was besieged;
despite brave resist-
ance, Warsaw fell in a
month.

The Germans
terrorised the local
population with ar-
rests, executions and
deportations, and a
Jewish ghetto was
constructed in 1940.
The city's residents

rebelled twice; first
came an eruption in
the Jewish ghetto in
April 1943, followed by
the general Warsaw
Rising in August 1944.
Both revolts were
cruelly crushed.

At the end of the
war, the city lay in ru-
ins and 800,000 peo-
ple – more than half of
the prewar population
– had perished. By
comparison, the total
military casualties
for US forces in WWII
was 400,000, for UK
forces 326,000. A
2004 historical com-
mission estimated

that the city suffered
in the region of $54.6
billion in losses during
the war.

Redeveloping
the Warsaw
Citadel

The Polish govern-
ment is building
not one but two
major museums in
the grounds of the
Warsaw Citadel. The
new **Polish History
Museum** (http://mu
zhp.pl) and the relo-
cated and enlarged
Polish Army Museum
(p110) are set to be

FOTOKON/GETTY IMAGES ©

completed by 2021. The pentagonal-shaped, red-brick Citadel was originally built as an army garrison and political prison in the mid-19th century during imperial Russian rule of Poland. Its redevelopment will also feature over 30 hectares of parkland and a central square.

The Katyń Museum (p55) occupies the southern section of the Citadel, while a wing of the old prison has been turned into the Museum of the X Pavilion of the Warsaw Citadel (p55).

Best Historical Sights

Warsaw Rising Museum All-encompassing account of the tragic events of the uprising against the 1944 German occupation. (pictured left; p84)

Museum of Warsaw Explore aspects of the city's history through the imaginative 'Things of Warsaw'–themed rooms. (p40)

Marie Skłodowska-Curie Museum The life and works of Nobel Prize–winning Curie are covered in the building in which she grew up. (pictured right; p50)

Katyń Museum Learn about the massacre of Polish military officers in the forests of Katyń in 1940 at this new museum in the Warsaw Citadel. (p55)

Praga Museum of Warsaw View long-hidden murals in an old, on-site set of Jewish prayer rooms. (p128)

Jewish Heritage

Jews have lived in Warsaw since at least the early 15th century. By 1939 the city had the largest Jewish population in the world after New York City, but its immense cultural and economic contribution couldn't save it from the Holocaust. All of which makes the tentative revival of Jewish life in contemporary Warsaw remarkable.

PAVEL STASEVICH/SHUTTERSTOCK ©

Community Revival

Anti-Semitic campaigns during Poland's communist years threatened to hammer the final nails in Jewish Warsaw's coffin. However, in recent times there have been many positive changes in connection with the city's past and present Jewish heritage.

The Nożyk Synagogue holds regular services (if you wish to attend one, it's necessary to contact the synagogue in advance). Much has also been done to preserve the city's two major Jewish cemeteries. JCC Warszawa offers a variety of Jewish cultural classes and activities, including Hebrew courses, and there's a busy program of annual events featuring Jewish music, food and film festivals.

Tracing Roots

Many Jewish visitors head to Warsaw to trace family roots in Poland. Good places to start digging into the past are POLIN and the Jewish Historical Institute, which offers a genealogy service with a free first consultation. Before making contact, search for as much detail on your family as you can, including checking online databases such as www. familysearch.org.

Festivals & Events

On 19 April, the anniversary of the Warsaw Ghetto Uprising, paper daffodil badges are distributed around Warsaw – a reference to Marek Edelman (1919–2009), one of the few survivors of the uprising, who used to lay a bouquet

GRAND WARSZAWSKI/SHUTTERSTOCK ©

of the flowers every year at the Monument to the Ghetto Heroes.

Held annually since 2004, **Singer's Warsaw Festival** (www.festiwalsingera.pl; late Aug-early Sep) includes Jewish-related theatre, music, films, exhibits and workshops at various city locations, including the Nożyk Synagogue, the Jewish Theatre and the Austrian Cultural Forum.

Best Jewish Sights

POLIN Museum of the History of Polish Jews A beacon of education and collective memory. (p86)

Jewish Historical Institute View a unique collection of direct testimonies about the extermination of Polish Jewry. (p66)

Jewish Cemetery Packed with a wide range of artistic tombstones and memorials to WWII victims. (pictured left; p91)

Nożyk Synagogue Beautifully restored and the only Warsaw synagogue to survive WWII. (p70)

Żabiński's' Villa Inside the city zoo, this house safely harboured Jews during WWII. (p130)

Bródno Jewish Cemetery The incredibly moving last resting place of Praga's Jews. (p128)

Online Resources

o Jewish Warsaw (http://warsze.polin.pl/en)

o My Jewish Warsaw (www.varshe.org.pl)

o Jewish Community of Warsaw (http://warszawa.jewish.org.pl)

Art & Design

ARCHITECT ADOLF KRISCHANITZ_
IRENA IRIS SZEWCZYK/SHUTTERSTOCK ©

Varsovians down the ages have had a keen eye for art and design. The Polish kings commissioned foreign artists to decorate their palaces, but by the middle of the 19th century, Poland was ready for its own painters. Communist times brought their own socialist realist aesthetic, most dazzlingly in the form of vivid neon signs.

Canaletto

Italian Bernardo Bellotto (c 1721–80), the nephew (and pupil) of that quintessential Venetian artist, Canaletto, became a court painter in Warsaw during the reign of King Stanisław August Poniatowski; a room in the Royal Castle (p36) is devoted to his detailed landscapes, which proved invaluable as references during the reconstruction of the Old Town after WWII. Bellotto often signed his canvases 'de Canaletto', so is known in Poland simply as Canaletto.

Jan Matejko

By the middle of the 19th century, Poland was ready for its own painters. Jan Matejko (1838–93) created stirring canvases that glorified Poland's past achievements. His most famous work, *The Battle of Grunwald*, an enormous painting that depicts the famous victory of the united Polish, Lithuanian and Ruthenian forces over the Teutonic Knights in 1410, is displayed in Warsaw's National Museum (p106).

Best Galleries

Neon Museum Ensuring the lights don't go out on iconic communist-era neon signs. (p122)

National Museum Several centuries of top-quality Polish art and design are on display in the country's largest museum. (p106)

Zachęta – National Gallery of Art Shows of contemporary works from local and international artists feature at this eminent institution. (p68)

Museum on the Vistula View Poland's largest painting on the exterior of this contemporary art gallery. (pictured; p68)

Entertainment

TUPUNGATO/SHUTTERSTOCK ©

Warsaw is home to many classical music, opera and performing arts venues. Polish theatre has long been enthusiastically supported in the capital, and the theatres stage top-class productions that are worth making time to see. Film is also well represented at both mainstream and art-house cinemas.

What's On

If it's the soccer season, consider heading to Legia Warsaw (p116) to cheer on the local football team Legia Warsaw, one of the most successful in the Polish league.

Up-to-date English-language entertainment listings are included on the websites of **Warsaw Insider** (www.warsaw insider.pl) and **Warsaw In Your Pocket** (www.inyourpocket. com/warsaw).

Best Classical Music

Teatr Wielki As well as opera you can see top-class ballet and classical music concerts at this grand theatre. (p78)

Filharmonia Narodowa From major symphonic concerts to jazz recitals, this is Warsaw's premier space for live music (p78)

Warszawa Opera Kameralna Best known for its productions of Mozart operas. (p98)

Best Theatre

Teatr Dramatyczny This much-respected theatre company is part of the Palace of Culture & Science. (pictured; p61)

Teatr Powszechny A chance to see excellent Polish theatre with English captions in Praga. (p134)

Best Live Music

Stodoła A hub for jazz music since the 1950s, this versatile venue features all genres of live music. (p117)

Hydrozagadka The largest venue in a street-art decorated courtyard in Praga has concerts by both local and international musicians. (p134)

For Kids

OLESIA BILKEI/SHUTTERSTOCK ©

Warsaw does a good job of entertaining children of all ages. The major museums are all very child friendly and creative in their approach to engaging young minds and hearts. Parks abound and in warmer months there are beaches along the Vistula as well as boat trips across and along the river.

Practicalities

Almost all city buses and trams have special areas to accommodate prams and pushchairs. Many restaurants cater for children with play areas, high chairs, and children's menus (*menu dla dzieci* or *menu dziecięce*). Children get discounts on local transport, accommodation and museum admission fees; museums often have child-friendly play areas. Nappies and toddlers' supplies are readily available in pharmacies, corner shops and supermarkets.

More Information

The city's tourist information offices offer a colourful, fold-out *Free Map for Young Travellers* aimed primarily at teens and students, but with some hints for younger travellers as well. For more ideas, see Kids in the City (http://kidsinthecity.pl).

Best Kid-Friendly Attractions

Copernicus Science Centre Wonderful interactive museum which also includes a great Planetarium. (p66)

Palace of Culture & Science The view from the observation tower is just the start of many offerings here aimed at entertaining kids and families. (p60)

Łazienki Park Plenty of space to run, plus peacocks to spot, ducks to feed and a boat trip to take. (p102)

Warsaw Zoological Gardens Plenty of outdoor enclosures to explore. (p128)

Filharmonia Narodowa Puts on regular concerts for children. (p78)

LGBT+

STUDIOFLARA/SHUTTERSTOCK ©

Warsaw's City Hall is committed to supporting LGBT+ rights and initiatives. There are LGBT+ bars and clubs in Warsaw and they're not too difficult to find. That said, many Poles are conservative and not accepting of gay culture, so use caution in showing same-sex affection in public.

Local Attitudes

Homosexuality is legal in Poland. However, the ruling Law & Justice (PiS) party is very anti-LGBT+ in its policies. This said, in Warsaw, you'll encounter a much more liberal attitude from most people. In March 2019, the city's mayor Rafał Trzaskowski signed a declaration promising an LGBT+ hostel and community centre, a local crisis intervention system, and access to anti-discrimination and sex education at schools – all things that the right-wing national government opposes.

What's On

Held in most years since 2001, the colourful **Equality Parade** (Parada Równości; www.paradarownosci.eu; ☺Jun) passes through the city's streets in mid-June in support of social equality and diversity. In 2018 it attracted some 45,000 spectators and supporters.

An occasional gay dance night is Revolution (www.facebook.com/revolution warsaw), held at different venues across the city. For more information on LGBT+ Warsaw, see https://queerintheworld.com/gay-warsaw-poland-travel-guide and https://queer.pl (in Polish only).

Best LGBT+ Venues

BarStudio Welcoming to everyone on the sexual/gender spectrum, also hosting occasional LGBT+ events. (p74)

Metropolis Muscled, topless bar staff and drag queens keep it glam at this weekend gay dance club. (p77)

Galeria Long-running, gay-friendly bar and DJ club beneath Hala Mirowska. (p77)

Four Perfect Days

Day 1

Start at the **Royal Castle** (p36), rebuilt like most of the rest of the Old Town following WWII. Learn about the city's history at the **Museum of Warsaw** (p40).

Lunch at **Warszawski Sznyt** (p50), overlooking Castle Sq. Spend the afternoon at the **POLIN Museum of the History of Polish Jews** (pictured; p86) in an amazing contemporary building at the heart of the former ghetto. There's much to see in this excellent museum but, if you have time, also take a stroll through the historic **Jewish Cemetery** (p91).

Attend an early evening piano recital at **Best of Chopin Concerts** (p53). After dinner at **U Fukiera** (p50) take a romantic walk around the Old Town's cobblestone streets.

Day 2

After breakfast at **Cafe Bristol** (p73) stroll down to the **Church of the Holy Cross** (p63), where Chopin's heart is interred. Learn more about the composer at the **Fryderyk Chopin Museum** (pictured; p58). Grab lunch at **SAM Powiśle** (p73). Cross the river to Praga – discover all about this working-class neighbourhood's fascinating history at the **Praga Museum of Warsaw** (p128) and be dazzled by the **Neon Museum** (p122) at the Soho Factory complex.

Book an early evening tour of the **Polish Vodka Museum** (p132), check out the watering and dining holes of the surrounding **Koneser complex** (p132), then bar hop along ul Ząbkowska.

ARCHITECT: RAINER MAHLAMAKI; PIOTRBB/SHUTTERSTOCK ©

OLIAGROVENKO/SHUTTERSTOCK ©

Day 3

AGE FOTOSTOCK/ALAMY STOCK PHOTO ©

Spend the morning immersed in Polish art and cultural treasures at the **National Museum** (p106), then admire the socialist realist architecture of **Plac Konstytucji** (p110). **Hala Koszyki** (pictured; p114) is packed with lunch options.

In the afternoon, stroll around magnificent **Łazienki Park** (p102), home also to the gorgeous art collection and beautiful interiors of the **Palace on the Isle** (p103) and the **Old Orangery** (p104).

At dusk head to the 30th-floor observatory deck in the **Palace of Culture & Science** (p60). For dinner try **Alewino** (p114) or **Youmiko Vegan Sushi** (p112), followed by hanging out with Warsaw's cool crowd in **Cafe Kulturalna** (p61) or **BarStudio** (p74).

Day 4

VIVOOO/SHUTTERSTOCK ©

Travel south of the city centre to **Wilanów Palace** (pictured; p138) and park. The original 17th-century palace is gorgeous, with each successive owner having adding different architectural and interior design styles. Enjoy lunch in the retro 1960s ambience of **Restauracja Wilanów** (p139).

Return to central Warsaw and devote several hours at least to the amazingly detailed exhibitions at the **Warsaw Rising Museum** (p84). Book ahead for dinner at **Bez Gwiazdek** (p73) or a night at the opera or ballet at **Teatr Wielki** (p78). If you prefer less formal entertainment, there are plenty of options down along the **Vistulan Boulevards** (p78).

Need to Know

For detailed information, see Survival Guide (p143)

Population
1.76 million

Currency
Polish złoty (zł)

Language
Polish

Visas
Generally not required for stays of up to 90 days.

Money
ATMs are fairly common. Credit cards are generally accepted and often preferred to cash.

Mobile Phones
Poland uses the GSM 900/1800 system.

Time
Central European Time (GMT/UTC plus one hour)

Tipping
Customary in restaurants, cafes and at service establishments such as hairdressers; optional elsewhere.

Daily Budget

Budget: Less than 200zł
Hostel dorm bed: 65zł
Meals in milk bars and self-catering: 40zł
Day pass for local transport: 15zł

Midrange: 200–600zł
Double room in a midrange hotel: 400zł
Meal in a midrange restaurant: 100zł
Museum tickets: 10–30zł

Top end: More than 600zł
Double room in a top hotel: 800zł
Meal in an upscale restaurant: 300zł
Ticket for opera: 200zł

Advance Planning

Three months before Search online for the best deals on flights and accommodation, especially if you're visiting during the busy summer season.

One month before Book tickets for popular attractions such as Wilanów Palace and Copernicus Science Centre. Do similarly for tickets at Filharmonia Narodowa and Teatr Wielki.

One week before Check out upcoming entertainment, festivals and events and make plans accordingly.

Arriving in Warsaw

Warsaw Chopin Airport Both trains (4.40zł, every 30 minutes to every hour, 20 minutes) and buses (4.40zł, every 15 minutes, 30 minutes) run to the city centre. Taxis cost 35zł to 50zł and take 20 to 30 minutes.

Warsaw Modlin Airport Frequent buses (ticket on board bus/in advance 35/9zł) take around 55 minutes to central Warsaw. For the train, ride the shuttle bus to Modlin station (19zł, one hour, at least hourly). Taxis cost 159zł between 6am and 10pm, 199zł at other times and take 30 to 40 minutes.

Warszawa Centralna Most central train station and terminus for intercity and international services. Well connected by buses, trains and taxis to other parts of the city. Closest metro stations are Centrum (Line 1) and Rondo ONZ (Line 2).

Getting Around

Ⓜ **Metro**

Two efficient lines provide access across Warsaw, but distances between stations can be long.

🚋🚌 **Tram & Bus**

Extensive network of both modes of transport often running alongside each other across the city. There are also night buses.

🚆 **Train**

Local trains can also be used for crossing the city, most handily between two sides of the Vistula and out to the airports.

🚗 **Taxi**

Best to book ahead than hail on the street; most people use apps such as Taxify and Uber.

🚲 **Bicycle**

A public bike-rental system is available from March to November. There are cycle lanes across much of the city.

AGSAZ/SHUTTERSTOCK ©

Warsaw Neighbourhoods

Żoliborz (p54)

Old Town & New Town (p35)

Destroyed at the end of WWII, Warsaw's Old Town has been atmospherically recreated. The adjacent New Town's quieter streets are home to monuments and museums.

POLIN Museum of the History of Polish Jews

Warsaw Rising Museum

Palace of Culture & Science

Muranów, Mirów & Powązki (p83)

These two residential and largely uncommercial districts are where the Germans created the Warsaw Ghetto in 1940; today scattered remnants of Jewish Warsaw survive.

Łazienki Park & Southern Śródmieście (p101)

The prime focus of this southern slice of Warsaw is lush Łazienki Park. Southern Śródmieście is home to the city's boldest socialist realist architecture.

Warsaw Chopin (4.5km)

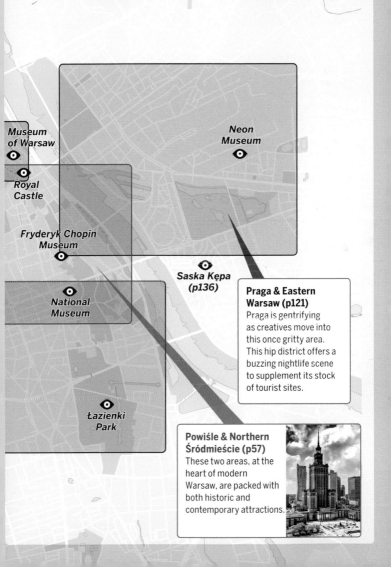

Museum
of Warsaw
⊙

⊙
Royal
Castle

Neon
Museum
⊙

Fryderyk Chopin
Museum
⊙

⊙
National
Museum

⊙
Saska Kępa
(p136)

**Praga & Eastern
Warsaw (p121)**
Praga is gentrifying
as creatives move into
this once gritty area.
This hip district offers a
buzzing nightlife scene
to supplement its stock
of tourist sites.

⊙
Łazienki
Park

**Powiśle & Northern
Śródmieście (p57)**
These two areas, at the
heart of modern
Warsaw, are packed with
both historic and
contemporary attractions.

Explore
Warsaw

Worth a Trip 🔭

Warsaw's Walking Tours 🥾

Syrenka statue, Old Town Square (p46) BART SADOWSKI/SHUTTERSTOCK ©

Explore
Old Town & New Town

All but destroyed at the end of WWII, the atmospheric cobble-streeted recreation of Warsaw's Old Town (Stare Miasto) includes the historic Royal Castle and St John's Cathedral as well as the beautiful Old Town Sq and superb Museum of Warsaw. The adjacent, and generally quieter New Town (Nowe Miasto), is home to the Marie Skłodowska-Curie Museum and the Monument to the Warsaw Rising.

The Short List

○ **Royal Castle (p36)** *Wandering through the gilded ensemble of rooms, bedecked with original art.*

○ **Museum of Warsaw (p40)** *Learning about the city's history from a fascinating collection curated along different themes.*

○ **Monument to the Warsaw Rising (p46)** *Saluting the brave, doomed heroes from the people's uprising of 1944.*

○ **Maria Skłodowska-Curie Museum (p50)** *Touring the birth home of the Nobel Prize–winning scientist.*

○ **Field Cathedral of the Polish Army (p48)** *Paying respects to Poland's fallen warriors at this elegantly decorated church.*

Getting There & Around

🚋 Services 4, 13, 20, 23, 26 and 28 stop at Stare Miasto.

🚌 Services 160, 190 and 527, plus night buses N11, N21, N61 and N71, stop at Stare Miasto. Plac Krasińkich is served by buses 116, 178, 180, 503 and 518 and is handy for sights in the New Town.

Old Town & New Town Map on p44

Old Town shopfront ANTONISTOCK/GETTY IMAGES ©

Top Sight 📷
Royal Castle

This massive brick edifice, a remarkable copy of the original blown up by the Germans in WWII, is filled with authentic period furniture and original artworks. It began life in the 14th century as a wooden stronghold of the dukes of Mazovia and evolved into one of Europe's most splendid royal palaces in the 17th century.

◉ MAP P44, F7

Zamek Królewski

www.zamek-krolewski.pl

adult/concession 30/20zł, free Wed

🕙 10am-6pm Tue-Thu & Sat, to 8pm Fri, 11am-6pm Sun, closes 4pm Oct-Apr

🚊 Stare Miasto

Great Assembly Hall

The castle's interior has largely been restored to its heyday in the 17th and 18th centuries. The standard tour begins on the 1st floor with the **Great Apartments** (rooms 1 to 9), created during the reign of Stanisław August Poniatowski and including the magnificent **Great Assembly Hall** with dazzling gilded stucco and golden columns. The enormous ceiling painting, *The Disentanglement of Chaos,* is a postwar recreation of a work by Marcello Bacciarelli showing King Stanisław bringing order to the world. The king's face also appears in a marble medallion above the main door, flanked by the allegorical figures of Peace and Justice.

National Hall & Marble Hall

The neighbouring **National Hall** was conceived by the king as a national pantheon; the six huge canvases (surviving originals) depict pivotal scenes from Polish history. A door leads off the hall into the smaller **Marble Room**, decorated in 16th century style with coloured marble and trompe l'oeil paintwork. The room houses 22 portraits of Polish kings, from Bolesław Chrobry to a large gilt-framed image of Stanisław August Poniatowski himself.

Throne Room & King's Apartments

The lavishly decorated **Throne Room** (pictured) is connected by a short corridor to the **King's Apartments** (rooms 11 to 20), the highlight of which is the **Canaletto Room**. An impressive array of 22 paintings by Bernardo Bellotto (1721–80) – the nephew of Italy's Canaletto, but who is best known in Poland by his uncle's name – captures Warsaw's mid-18th-century heyday in great detail. The works were of immense help in reconstructing the city's historic facades.

★ **Top Tips**

○ Entrance is free on Wednesday.

○ Buy tickets for the main castle rooms, special exhibitions, the Tin-Roofed Palace and guided tours (adult/concession 15/10zł) at the office on the right of the courtyard as you enter from Castle Sq.

✕ **Take a Break**

Inside the castle's main building is the frou-frou **Cafe Zamek** (https://www.cafe-zamek.pl), which includes a formal restaurant and a slightly more casual cafe.

The best view of the castle's exterior is from the stylish restaurant Warszawski Sznyt (p50), where you can have anything from breakfast to a late-night steak and cocktails.

Lanckoroński Collection

Back on the ground floor don't leave before looking at the Lanckoroński Collection. On display here are some of the 37 canvases donated to Poland in 1994 by Countess Karolina Lanckorońska, a remarkable Polish noblewoman who was a resistance fighter during WWII and survived Ravensbrück concentration camp to die in 2002 at the age of 104. The highlight is two portraits by Rembrandt – *Girl in a Picture Frame* and *Scholar at His Writing Table* – both of which you can go behind to see X-ray images of what lies beneath the paintings' surfaces.

Kubicki Arcades

Named after the architect Jakub Kubicki, these vaulted **arcades** (Arkady Kubickiego; admission free; ⊙10am-6pm, from 11am Sun) were constructed between 1819 and 1821 on the Vistula embankment beneath the castle. As well as the permanent exhibition, *The Royal Castle – from Destruction to Reconstruction*, they're used to host various exhibitions and events and are fronted by pleasant riverside gardens.

It's fun to climb the stairs through the brick-lined tunnel back up to the castle from the arcades.

Royal Castle from the grounds

Warsaw Rises

The first fortified settlements on the site of modern-day Warsaw appeared in the 9th and 10th centuries. In 1406 Janusz I moved his capital to Warsaw. Things went swimmingly for over a century until, in 1526, the last duke of Mazovia died without an heir. The burgeoning town – and the whole of Mazovia – fell under the direct rule of the king in Kraków and was incorporated into royal territory.

Warsaw's fortunes took a turn for the better after the unification of Poland and Lithuania in 1569, when the Sejm (the lower house of parliament) voted to make Warsaw the seat of its debates because of its central position in the new, larger country. The ultimate ennoblement came in 1596, when King Zygmunt III Waza decided to move his capital from Kraków to Warsaw.

The Swedish invasion from 1655 to 1660 was not kind to Warsaw, but the city recovered and continued to develop. Paradoxically, the 18th century – a period of catastrophic decline for the Polish state – witnessed Warsaw's greatest prosperity. A wealth of palaces and churches was erected, and cultural and artistic life flourished, particularly during the reign of the last Polish king, Stanisław August Poniatowski.

Tin-Roofed Palace

You need to exit the main complex and go around the south side of the building to find the entrance to this pretty, compact **palace** (Pałac Pod Blachą; ☎ 22 355 5170; adult/concession 15/10zł, free Wed; ☉10am-4pm Tue-Sat, from 11am Sun Oct-Apr, 10am-6pm Mon-Sat, from 11am Sun May-Sep).

The official English name isn't entirely correct as the palace is roofed with copper, one of the first such 17th-century buildings in Warsaw to use the metal in this way. It offers two exhibitions: the carpets and woven arts collection of the Teresa Sahakian Foundation (ground floor); and the apartments of Prince Józef Poniatowski (1st floor).

Top Sight 📷
Museum of Warsaw

Occupying 11 tenement houses on the north side of the Old Town Sq, this superb museum tells Warsaw's dramatic history in innovative ways. Although there is much to see here, it's also worth making time to visit the museum's other branches around the Old Town: the Heritage Interpretation Centre, the Museum of Pharmacy and the Barbican.

◎ **MAP P44, D5**

Muzeum Warszawy

www.muzeumwarszawy.pl

adult/concession 20/15zł, free Thu

⊘10am-7pm Tue-Sun

🚊Stare Miasto

Heritage Interpretation Centre

At the end of WWII the Old Town was mostly piles of rubble. To gain a full appreciation of the mammoth and heroic effort needed to reconstruct the historic area, a visit to this branch of the museum is highly recommended. The exhibition is compact and has excellent English explanations.

Museum of Pharmacy

Officially named after the Master of Pharmacy and women's rights campaigner Antonina Leśniewska (1866–1937), this charming little museum is devoted to the history of traditional pharmacies, which not only sold medicines but also produced them. The walnut wooden shop fixtures in the first exhibition hall are exquisite and display medicines bottles in all shapes and colours. A small exhibition covers *kampo* – Japanese traditional medicines.

The Barbican

This semicircular defensive tower (pictured) topped with a decorative Renaissance parapet is part of the medieval fortifications surrounding the Old Town. It was partially dismantled in the 19th century but reconstructed after WWII – something you can learn all about in the exhibition inside the red-brick tower which covers the history of the Old Town walls.

★ Top Tips

○ All branches of the museum are free to visit on Thursday.

○ The museum's Kino Syrena cinema screens the 70-minute documentary *The River of Treasures* from Tuesday to Thursday at 5pm; at other times you can ask the staff to screen the 20-minute documentary *Warsaw Will Not Forget*.

○ Return on Friday and Saturday evenings to watch global art-house movies, some in English.

○ The path running through the Barbican is a popular spot for buskers and art and craft sellers.

✕ Take a Break

The museum's **Lapidarium Cafe** (☑538 456 777; www.lapidariumcafe.com; Rynek Starego Miasta 40, Stare Miasto; ☉10am-7pm Tue-Sun; 🚊Stare Miasto) is a cosy, modern spot for a drink or a snack.

Walking Tour 🚶

Around Old Town

Nearly every building in the Old Town was reconstructed after being reduced to rubble by the Germans at the close of WWII. On this walk around its atmospheric cobbled streets you'll encounter a beguiling blend of Renaissance, baroque, Gothic and neoclassical elements that collectively make up the city's finest architectural ensemble.

Walk Facts

Start Viewing Terrace

End Castle Sq

Length 1.5km; two to four hours.

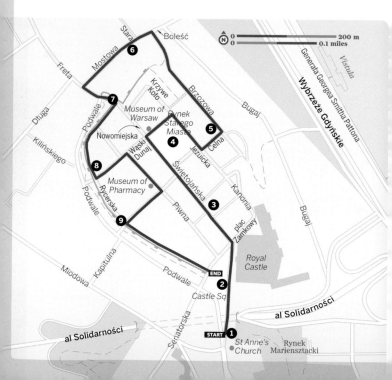

❶ Viewing Terrace

For a bird's-eye preview of the Old Town, it's worth climbing the 148 steps of the bell tower of **St Anne's Church** (Taras Widokowy; Krakowskie Przedmieście 68, Śródmieście Północne; adult/concession 6/5zł; ⏱10am-6pm Mon-Fri, 11am-8pm Sat & Sun; 🚃 Stare Miasto).

❷ Sigismund's Column

Piercing Castle Sq is this **column** (Kolumna Zygmunta) topped by a statue of Sigismund III Vasa, originally erected by the king's son, Władysław Vasa, in 1644.

❸ St John's Cathedral

Turn off Castle Sq into ul Świętojańska to reach this cathedral (p47), Warsaw's mother church.

❹ Old Town Square

In the centre of picturesque Old Town Sq (p46) stands a statue of *Syrenka*, the fierce mermaid brandishing a sword that's become a symbol of the city.

❺ Heritage Interpretation Centre

Drop into the **Heritage Interpretation Centre** (☎22 635 3402; www.muzeumwarszawy.pl; ul Brzozowa 11/13, Stare Miasto; adult/concession 5/3zł; ⏱10am-7pm Tue-Sun, free Thu; 🚃 Stare Miasto), whose exhibition provides a great insight into the mammoth effort needed to reconstruct the Old Town after WWII.

❻ 1950s Mosaics

Covering much of the end of the tenement building, this striking ceramic-tile **mosaic** (ul Mostowa 9a, Nowe Miasto; 🚃 Stare Miasto), designed in 1956 by Zofia Czarnocka-Kowalska, combines classical Greek poses with socialist realist art to depict heroic men and women at work and play. Nearby, look for the more avant-garde 1950s mosaic design by Roman Artymowski on the building at ul Mostowa 2.

❼ Barbican

Check out the craftspeople and artists peddling their wares in the **Barbican** (Barbakan; ul Nowomiejska, Stare Miasto; adult/concession 5/3zł; ⏱10am-6pm Tue-Sun May–mid-Aug; 🚃 Stare Miasto).

❽ Little Insurgent Monument

Continue around the fortress walls to find this poignant **monument** (Mały Powstaniec; Podwale, Stare Miasto; 🚃 Stare Miasto) commemorating the child soldiers who fought and died during the Warsaw Rising.

❾ Jan Kiliński Monument

Check out this **monument** (Pomnik Jana Kilińskiego; ul Piekarska 20, Stare Miasto; 🚃 Stare Miasto) to the hero of the 1794 Kościuszko Uprising then follow the old fortress walls back to Castle Sq.

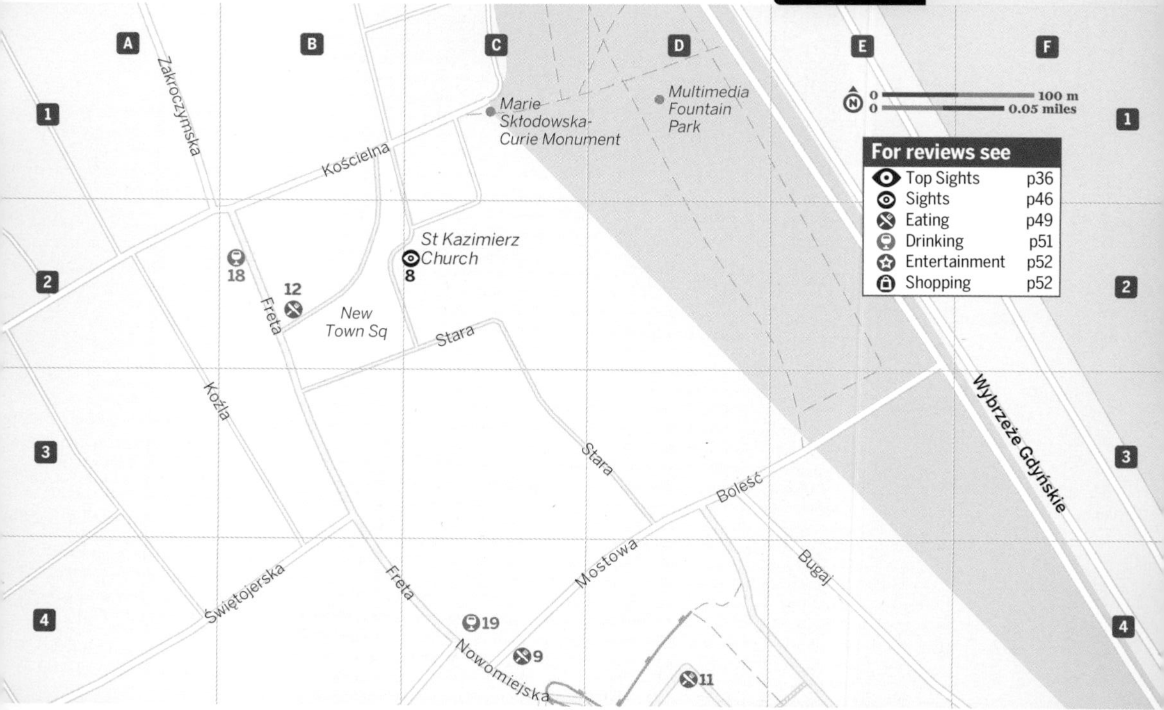

Old Town & New Town

N
0 — 100 m
0 — 0.05 miles

Marie-Skłodowska-Curie Monument

Multimedia Fountain Park

St Kazimierz Church

New Town Sq

Wybrzeże Gdyńskie

Zakroczymska

Kościelna

Freta

Koźla

Stara

Stara

Freta

Bolęść

Mostowa

Nowomiejska

Bugaj

Świętojerska

12 ✕

18 🛈

◎ 8

19 ⊙

9 ✕

11 ✕

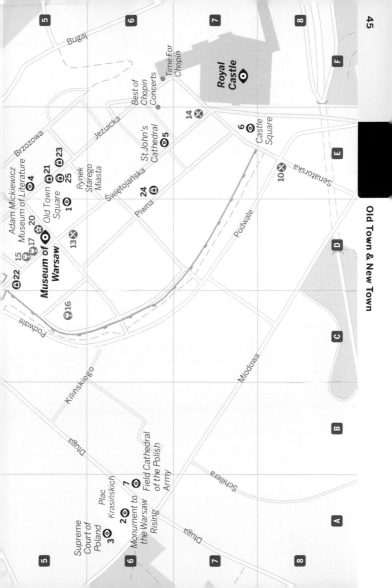

Bugaj

Time For Chopin

Best of Chopin Concerts

Royal Castle

F

Jezuicka

St John's Cathedral ◉5

14 ✕

Brzozowa

Museum of Literature
Adam Mickiewicz ✪
◉4

20
◉23
21
Old Town
Square
25
Rynek Starego Miasta
Świętojańska
◉1

Castle Square

6 ◉
E

Senatorska

10 ✕

22

15
17
Museum of Warsaw ◉

13 ✕

24

Piwna

Podwale

D

◉16

Podwale

C

Miodowa

Kilińskiego

Długa

B

Schillera

Supreme Court of Poland
3 ◉

Plac Krasińskich

2 ◉
7 ◉
Monument to the Warsaw Rising

Field Cathedral of the Polish Army

Długa

A

6

7

8

5

6

7

8

Sights

Old Town Square

SQUARE

1 ⊙ MAP P44, D5

For those with an eye for historic buildings this is Warsaw's loveliest square, not to mention its oldest, having been established at the turn of the 13th century. It's enclosed by around 40 tall houses exhibiting a fine blend of Renaissance, baroque, Gothic and neoclassical elements; aside from the facades at Nos 34 and 36, all were rebuilt after being reduced to rubble by the Germans at the close of WWII. (Rynek Starego Miasta, Stare Miasto; ⊟Stare Miasto)

Monument to the Warsaw Rising

MONUMENT

2 ⊙ MAP P44, A6

One of Warsaw's most important landmarks, this dynamic bronze tableau depicts Armia Krajowa (AK; Home Army) fighters emerging ghostlike from the shattered brickwork of their ruined city, while others descend through a manhole into the network of sewers. The monument was unveiled on 1 August 1989, the 45th anniversary of the doomed revolt against German military occupation in 1944. (Pomnik Powstania Warszawskiego; Plac Krasińskich, Nowe Miasto; ⊟Plac Krasińskich)

Tomb of the dukes of Mazovia, St John's Cathedral

LINDASKY76/SHUTTERSTOCK ©

Supreme Court of Poland

ARCHITECTURE

3 ◉ MAP P44, A6

Marek Budzyński was one of the architects responsible for this impressive building, completed in 2000. It features a facade of copper-clad columns decorated with maxims of Roman law. Go around the back of the building off ul Świętojerska to view three caryatids sculpted by Jerzy Jucz-kowicz symbolising the virtues of faith, hope and love. (Sąd Najwyższy; www.sn.pl; Plac Krasińskich 2-6, Nowe Miasto; 🚊 Plac Krasińskich)

Adam Mickiewicz Museum of Literature

MUSEUM

4 ◉ MAP P44, E5

Occupying two historic tenement buildings in the Old Town Sq, this museum does a good job of covering the life and times of Poland's national poet Adam Mickiewicz (1798–1855). The exhibition spans several rooms, includes some original manuscripts and paintings of the romantic poet, and has good English captions. (Muzeum Literatury im A Mickiewicza; 📞 22 831 4061; http://muzeumliteratury.pl; Rynek Starego Miasta 20, Stare Miasto; adult/concession 6/5zł; ⏰ 10am-4pm Mon, Tue, Fri, 11am-6pm Wed & Thu, 11am-5pm Sun; 🚊 Stare Miasto)

St John's Cathedral

CATHEDRAL

5 ◉ MAP P44, E6

Considered the oldest of Warsaw's churches, St John's was built at the beginning of the 15th century on the site of a wooden church, and subsequently remodelled several times. Razed during WWII, it regained its Gothic shape through postwar reconstruction. Look for the red-marble Renaissance tomb of the last dukes of Mazovia in the right-hand aisle, then go downstairs to the crypt to see more tombstones, including that of Nobel Prize–winning writer Henryk Sienkiewicz (1846–1916). (Archikatedra św Jana; 📞 22 831 0289; www.katedra.mkw.pl; ul Świętojańska 8, Stare Miasto; crypt 2zł; ⏰ 10am-1pm & 3-5.30pm Mon-Sat; 🚊 Stare Miasto)

Castle Square

SQUARE

6 ◉ MAP P44, E7

A natural spot from which to start exploring the Old Town is triangular Castle Sq. Attracting snap-happy tourists by the hundreds each day is the square's centrepiece, the **Sigismund's Column**. Free entertainment is provided by buskers here in the evenings and on weekends.

The 22m-high monument to Sigismund III Vasa, who moved the capital from Kraków to Warsaw, is modelled on the Italian columns that Władysław Vasa had seen on a visit to Rome in 1625. The granite column was knocked down during WWII, but the statue survived and was placed on a new column four years after the war. The original, shrapnel-scarred column now lies along the south wall of the Royal Castle. (Plac Zamkowy, Stare Miasto; 🚊 Stare Miasto)

Old & New Town Architecture

Warsaw's architectural history begins in the Old and New Towns, the oldest parts of the city. **St John's Cathedral** (p47) was originally built in the 14th century in Mazovian Gothic style and it was to this exterior design (not its altered pre-WWII appearance) that it was rebuilt in the 1950s. Consecrated in 1411, **St Mary's Church** (Kościół Mariacki; ✆ 22 831 2473; www.przyrynek.waw.pl; Przyrynek 2, Nowe Miasto; 🚊 Sanguszki) is one of Warsaw's few surviving examples of Gothic architecture. Over the centuries it has been demolished and rebuilt several times. Its characteristic bell tower (a 1518 addition to the church) can be seen in old paintings, including ones by Canaletto.

Completed in 1639, **St Hyacinth's Church** (Kościół św Jacka; ✆ 22 635 4700; https://freta.dominikanie.pl; ul Freta 10, Nowe Miasto; 🚊 Plac Krasińskich) is a mixture of Renaissance and early-baroque styles. The interior, which is more modern, is set below street level as the church stands on the sloping river bank. A prime example of late-Renaissance or mannerist architecture is the **Royal Castle** (p36), although sections of it are older and the complex was much altered in later centuries.

At the end of WWII, about 15% of the city was left standing. So complete was the destruction that there were even suggestions that the capital should be moved elsewhere, but instead it was decided that parts of the prewar urban fabric would be rebuilt. The most valuable historic monuments were restored to their previous appearance, based on original drawings and photographs. Between 1949 and 1963 work was concentrated on the Old Town, aiming to return it, more or less, to its 17th- and 18th-century appearance – today not a single building in the area looks less than 200 years old. So complete was the restoration that Unesco granted the Old Town World Heritage status in 1980.

Reconstruction of the Royal Castle began in 1971 and it took until 1984 for the splendid baroque building to be fully resurrected. Here, as elsewhere in the Old Town, many original architectural fragments were incorporated into the walls.

Field Cathedral of the Polish Army

CHURCH

7 ◉ MAP P44, A6

One of Warsaw's most interesting churches is this traditional place of worship for soldiers. There's no homage to the glory of war here; instead some impressive memorials and numerous plaques to fallen Polish soldiers, including a chapel dedicated to the thousands murdered in the Katyń Massacre and other incidents through WWII. Head to the crypt to find the small museum. (Katedra Polowa Wojska Polskiego; ☎261 877 702; www.katedrapolowa.pl; ul Długa 13/15, Nowe Miasto; adult/concession 5/2.50zł; ☉museum 10am-6pm Tue-Sun; 🚇Plac Krasińskich)

St Kazimierz Church CHURCH

8 ◉ MAP P44, C2

Attached to a monastery of Benedictine nuns, this interesting 17th-century church is the work of prominent architect Tylman van Gameren. It has a fine baroque exterior and a clean white interior. Used as a hospital for insurgents during WWII, and thus targeted for bombing by the Germans, the church was rebuilt in the 1950s.

(Kościół Sakramentek pw św Kazimierza; ☎22 831 4962; www.benedyktynki-sakramentki.org; Rynek Nowego Miasta 2, Novo Miasto; 🚇Plac Krasińskich)

Eating

Bar Mleczny Pod Barbakanem POLISH $

9 ✕ MAP P44, C4

Just outside the Barbican, look for this traditional milk bar (self-service canteen) that's been around for decades. Don't be put off by the faded exterior; it remains popular for Polish staples such as pierogi (dumplings) and pork chops. (☎22 831 4737; http://barpodbarbakanem.pl; ul Mostowa 27, Nowe Miasto; mains 7-10zł; ☉8am-4pm Mon-Fri, 9am-5pm Sat & Sun; 🖋; 🚇Plac Krasińskich)

Al fresco dining in the Old Town

UNDEFINED UNDEFINED/GETTY IMAGES ©

Maria Skłodowska-Curie

The first woman to win the Nobel Prize, Maria Skłodowska (Marie Curie) was born in Warsaw in 1867. Her original home, where she lived for her first 19 years, is now a small **museum** (Muzeum Marii Skłodowskiej-Curie; ☑22 831 8092; www.muzeum-msc.pl; ul Freta 16, Nowe Miasto; adult/concession 11/6zł; ⏱10am-7pm Tue-Sun Jun-Aug, 9am-4pm Tue-Sun rest of year; ⊡Plac Krasiński) chronicling the life and work of the distinguished scientist and displaying items from Pierre and Maria's laboratory as well as other memorabilia. Unfortunately, there are sparse English captions but there's enough here give you an idea of the woman's achievements.

A short walk away from the museum, an attractive contemporary statue of **Curie** (Monument Maria Skłodowska-Curie; Map p44, C1; ul Kościelna, Nowe Miasto; ⊡Sanguszki) overlooks the Vistula, a river she described as 'so enchanting, that I cannot even begin to describe it'.

Warszawski Sznyt   STEAK $$

10 🍴 MAP P44, E8

With a dress-circle view of Plac Zamkowy and the Royal Castle, this stylish, multilevel place is great for all-day dining. It specialises in steaks and burgers and also does a mean pastrami sandwich. (☑22 829 2050; https://warszawskisznyt.pl; ul Senatorska 2, Stare Miasto; mains 22-79zł; ⏱8am-11pm; ⊡Stare Miasto)

Sambal   INDONESIAN $$

11 🍴 MAP P44, D4

Bringing the tropical flavour and heat of Southeast Asia to the Old Town, Sambal is run by an Indonesian chef. His authentic versions of the salad *gado gado,* the rice dish *nasi goreng* and the beef and coconut milk stew *rendang padang* are all on the money. (☑22 635 0431; http://sambalrestaurant.pl; Krzywe Koło 1/3, Stare Miasto; mains 27-34zł; ⏱11am-9pm Tue-Fri & Sun, 10am-10pm Sat; 🛜; ⊡Stare Miasto)

Enoteca   POLISH $$$

12 🍴 MAP P44, B2

Classy, chic spot for good Polish and Italian food or a glass of wine, with a view onto the New Town's central square. In warmer months it has outdoor tables. (☑882 048 012; www.restauracjaenoteka.pl; Rynek Nowego Miasta 13/15, Nowe Miasto; mains 59-89zł; ⏱10am-10pm Sun-Thu, to 11pm Fri & Sat; ⊡Plac Krasińskich)

U Fukiera   POLISH $$$

13 🍴 MAP P44, D5

Polish cuisine is served simply but elegantly in this choice, antique Old Town spot, one in the stable of celeb restaurateur Magda Gessler.

The main dining room is all wood panelling and vaulted ceilings. There's also a cosy wine cellar and a lovely internal courtyard for dining in warmer weather. (☑22 831 1013; http://ufukiera.pl; Rynek Starego Miasta 27, Stare Miasto; mains 56-105zł; ⊙noon-midnight; 🛜; 🚃Stare Miasto)

Restauracja Polka POLISH $$$

14 🍴 MAP P44, E7

Magda Gessler loves to fit out her restaurants with folksy floral designs and rustic wooden tables, and this Old Town venue is no exception. High-quality versions of traditional Polish food issue from the kitchen, including blood sausage, pork shanks on cabbage, and crispy duck in honey. Some tables have views of Castle Sq. (☑22 635 3535; www.restauracjapolka.pl; ul Świętojańska 2, Stare Miasto; mains 32-72zł; ⊙noon-11pm; 🚃Stare Miasto)

Drinking

Same Fusy TEAHOUSE

15 🍵 MAP P44, D5

This brick-vaulted basement offers a romantic, candle-lit atmosphere in which to enjoy some 120 different types and flavours of tea and infusions. (☑22 635 9014; www.samefusy.pl; ul Nowomiejska 10, Stare Miasto; ⊙1-11pm; 🚃Stare Miasto)

Maryensztadt CRAFT BEER

16 🍵 MAP P44, C5

This award-winning craft brewery based in Zwoleń, a small town near

Forteca Kręgliccy Market

If you're looking for local culinary goodies to take home as gifts or to buy for yourself for a picnic, join locals at the weekly **Forteca Kręgliccy Market** (Map p44; www.facebook.com/pg/forteca.kregliccy; ul Zakroczymska 12, Nowe Miasto; ⊙8am-2pm Wed; 🚃Park Traugutta) held in the red-brick Fort Legionów, which was built by the Russians in the 1850s.

Warsaw, offers 15 of its beers on tap (plus a guest beer) and many more by the bottle. It's also a good place to eat a variety of Polish dishes (25zł to 59zł) that you can pair with its beers. (☑791 522 406; www.restauracjamaryensztadt.pl; ul Szeroki Dunja 11, Stare Miasto; ⊙noon-11pm Sun-Thu, to midnight Fri & Sat; 🚃Stare Miasto)

Same Krafty CRAFT BEER

17 🍵 MAP P44, D5

Split across two locations facing each other on opposite sides of the street, Same Krafty is a convivial spot to sample a wide variety of Polish craft beers accompanied by slices of pizza. (☑793 802 523; www.facebook.com/samekrafty; ul Nowomiejska 10, Stare Miasto; ⊙2-11pm Mon, from 1pm Tue & Wed, until midnight Thu & Sun, until 1am Fri & Sat; 🚃Stare Miasto)

Polyester
BAR

18 MAP P44, B2

Smooth establishment with retro furnishings and a laid-back vibe. Serves good cocktails, as well as a full range of coffee drinks and light food. (☏733 464 600; ul Freta 49/51, Nowe Miasto; ☉noon-12.30am Sun-Thu, to 1.30am Fri & Sat; ☏; ☐Plac Krasińskich)

Pożegnanie z Afryką
CAFE

19 MAP P44, C4

'Out of Africa' is a cosy cafe offering nothing much beyond coffee – but what coffee! Choose from around 50 varieties, served in a little pot, and a range of tempting cakes. (☏501 383 091; www.facebook.com/pozegnaniezafrykawawa; ul Freta 4/6, Nowe Miasto; ☉10am-7pm Mon-Fri, to 5pm Sat & Sun; ☐Plac Krasińskich)

Entertainment

Kino Syrena
CINEMA

20 MAP P44, D5

From Tuesday to Thursday at 5pm, the 70-minute documentary *The River of Treasures* about sculptures lying for 350 years at the bottom of the Vistula River is screened. At other times you can ask staff to see the 20-minute documentary *Warsaw Will Not Forget*. On Friday and Saturday evenings global art-house movies are screened, some in English. (☏22 277 4402; https://muzeumwarszawy.pl; Muzeum Warszawy, Rynek Starego Miasta 28-42, Stare Miasto; adult/concession 10/7zł; ☐Stare Miasto)

Shopping

Dom Sztuki Lodowej
GIFTS & SOUVENIRS

21 MAP P44, E5

One of the best and certainly the most colourful collections of

---

Multimedia Fountain Park

Cap a summer's evening stroll along the Old and New Town's cobbled lanes by attending the impressive sound and light shows at the **Multimedia Fountain Park** (Multimedialny Park Fontann; Map p44, D1; http://park-fontann.pl; skwer I Dywizji Pancernej, Nowe Miasto; admission free; ☉8.30am-10.30pm May-Sep; ☐Sanguszki). Arrive early to grab a good viewing spot – from mid-May to mid-August the shows start at 9.30pm, at other times 9pm – although it's best to check online as they are weather dependent.

There are also shorter, winter light shows held Friday to Sunday at 4pm, 5pm and 6pm from early December until the end of January.

Polish folk-art souvenirs in the Old Town. Across two floors you'll find good examples of everything from painted wood carvings to traditional costumes and pottery. (22 831 1805; www.epolart.pl; Rynek Starego Miasta 10, Stare Miasto; 10am-6pm Mon-Fri, to 4pm Sat, noon-4pm Sun; Stare Miasto)

Lapidarium ANTIQUES

22 MAP P44, D5

Every square inch of this Aladdin's Cave of a shop is packed with antiques and curios, including jewellery, folk and religious art, military medals, badges and uniforms, and tonnes of vintage postcards and photos. (509 601 894; www.lapidarium.pl; ul Nowomiejska 15/17, Stare Miasto; 10am-9pm; Stare Miasto)

Bursztynek JEWELLERY

23 MAP P44, E5

Shops selling jewellery, trinkets and *objets d'art* made from Baltic amber are common around the Old Town. This one on Central Sq offers a wide range of products at various price points, and has the advantage of an interesting small free museum upstairs explaining how amber is produced from the fossilised resin of coniferous trees. (506 007 685; www.bursztynek.co; Rynek Starego Miasta 4/6, Stare Miasto; 10am-8pm; Stare Miasto)

Polish Poster Gallery ART

24 MAP P44, E6

Living up to its name, the Polish Poster Gallery stocks a broad col-

Chopin Concerts

Each evening intimate piano recitals are given at both the **Best of Chopin Concerts** (www.chopinconcerts.pl; Warsaw Archdiocese Museum; adult/concession 45zł; 6.30pm) or **Time For Chopin** (https://timeforchopin.eu; ZPAF Old Gallery; 60zł; 6pm); the performers are virtuosos who have played at major venues around the world. The recitals last an hour, including a short break.

lection of locally produced posters, both originals and cheaper new prints. A touchscreen catalogue of its wares makes it easy to browse the options, which include movie, theatre, circus and music posters. (Galeria Plakatu; 516 830 525; www.poster.com.pl; ul Piwna 28/30, Stare Miasto; 10am-8pm Sun-Thu, to 9pm Fri & Sat; Stare Miasto)

Metal Marcin Zaremski JEWELLERY

25 MAP P44, E5

Geometric designs are a hallmark of the gold-plated silver jewellery by designer Marcin Zaremski. You'll also find creations here by other designers including contemporary pieces made with amber. (22 831 6481; http://zaremski.pl; Rynek Starego Miasta 8, Stare Miasto; noon-4pm Wed, to 5pm Mon, Tue & Thu-Sat; Stare Miasto)

Walking Tour 🥾

Żoliborz

A delightful area to explore on foot or bicycle is Żoliborz, which derives its name from joli bord, French for 'beautiful embankment'. During Russian imperial rule, the Warsaw Citadel was built here, while in the early 20th century estates of neoclassical and modernist homes were created to house the city's intelligentsia and elites.

Walk Facts

Start Most Gdański tram or bus stop

End Plac Wisona metro station

Length 4km; four hours

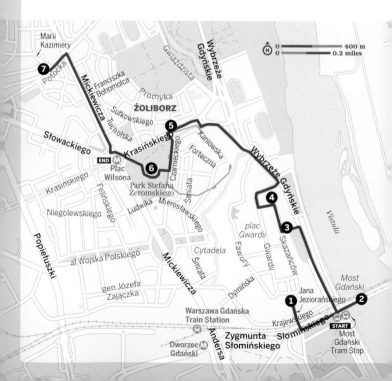

❶ Katyń Museum

This fine **museum** (Muzeum Katyńskie; www.muzeumkatynskie.pl; Warsaw Citadel, ul Jana Jeziorańskiego 4; admission free; ⊙10am-5pm Wed, to 4pm Thu-Sun) is devoted to the massacre of Polish military officers in the forests of Katyń in 1940, and all other victims of Soviet aggression during WWII. The detailed displays leave no stone unturned on the tragic events.

❷ Gdański Bridge

Stroll along the pedestrian promenade that runs under the Gdański Bridge, looking up to see the neon sign **MIŁO CIĘ WIDZIEĆ**. Meaning 'It's Nice to See You', this was the winner of a 2013 competition to design a new symbol for the city.

❸ Brama Straceń

Brama Straceń (Lost Gate; Wybrzeże Gdyńskie), the eastern gate to the Warsaw Citadel, was where political prisoners were executed in the late 19th century. In their memory, over 100 stone crosses and several Jewish tombstones stand on the embankment here.

❹ Museum of the X Pavilion of the Warsaw Citadel

Highlights of this **museum** (X Pawilon Cytadeli Warszawskiej; http://muzeum-niepodleglosci.pl/xpawilon; ul Skazańców 25; adult/concession 8/5zł, Thu free; ⊙10am-5pm Wed-Sun) in the old jail of Warsaw Citadel are the paintings by former inmate Alexander Sochaczewski (1843–1923), including the epic *Pożegnanie Europy* (Farewell to Europe).

❺ Spotkanie

Elegantly old-fashioned **restaurant** (www.spotkanie.com.pl; ul Krasińskiego 2; mains 25-39zł; ⊙noon-11pm Mon-Sat, to 10pm Sun; 🛜) specialises in classic Polish dishes such as the sour rye soup *żurek*, beef tartare and roast duck with apple, all served in hearty portions.

❻ Prochownia Żoliborz

Appreciate the leafy ambience of Park Żeromskiego at the cafe-bar **Prochownia Żoliborz** (http://prochowniazoliborz.com; ul Czarnieckiego 51; ⊙10am-midnight Sun-Thu, to 1am Fri & Sat; 🛜). It serves a good range of drinks and nibbles and hosts events including DJs and open-air cinema screenings.

❼ Bowie Mural

This **mural** (Marii Kazimiery 1) of the singer in his Ziggy Stardust persona was unveiled in 2016 on the 40th anniversary of David Bowie's legendary brief visit to Żoliborz during a train journey he and Iggy Pop were taking between Berlin and Moscow.

Explore

Powiśle & Northern Śródmieście

These two areas are packed with historic and contemporary attractions not least of which is the monumental Palace of Culture & Science. Powiśle hugs the west embankment of the Vistula. Northern Śródmieście (Śródmieście Północne) occupies the high ground and includes the start of the Royal Way, running down Krakowskie Przedmieście.

The Short List

○ **Palace of Culture & Science (p60)** *Taking in the city skyline from the 30th-floor observation deck of this iconic building.*

○ **Fryderyk Chopin Museum (p58)** *Listening to the music of Warsaw's favourite son in this high-tech museum that charts his life.*

○ **Copernicus Science Centre (p66)** *Having fun while learning about all aspects of science.*

○ **Jewish Historical Institute (p66)** *Reading heartbreaking texts from the World Heritage–listed Ringelblum Archive.*

○ **Vistulan Boulevards (p78)** *Strolling along this attractively designed riverside promenade.*

Getting There & Around

Ⓜ Lines 1 and 2 intersect at Świętokrzyska; other handy stations for the area include Centrum, Ratusz Arsenał, Nowy Świat-Uniwersytet and Centrum Nauki Kopernik.

Ⓣ Lines 4, 15, 18 and 35 run along ul Marszałkowska, lines 2, 7, 9, 24 and 25 along al Jerozolimskie.

Powiśle & Northern Śródmieście Map on p64

Palace of Culture & Science (p60) MICHAL BEDNAREK/500PX ©

Top Sight 📷
Fryderyk Chopin Museum

This multimedia museum within the Ostrogski Palace showcases the work of Poland's most famous composer and contain's the world's largest collection of his memorabilia. You're encouraged to take your time through four floors of displays, including stopping by the listening booths in the basement where you can browse Chopin's oeuvre to your heart's content.

◎ MAP P64, F4

https://muzeum.nifc.pl/pl

ul Okólnik 1, Śródmieście Północne

adult/concession 22/13zł, Wed free

🕐 11am-8pm Tue-Sun

Ⓜ Nowy Świat-Uniwersytet

All About Chopin

The Ostrogski Palace, rebuilt in the 1950s to the original 17th-century design of Tylman van Gameren, houses this impressive museum that performs a virtuoso task of crafting a thorough overview of Chopin's life and times from his birth in Żelazowa Wola to his death in Paris in 1849. Original letters, sketches, paintings as well as the composer's Pleyel grand piano, used during the final two years of his life, and his death mask are part of a collection that will thrill Chopin fans. Modern bells and whistles include touchscreen displays, a children's activities room and listening booths in the basement where you can access recordings of his music.

Chopin in Warsaw

Chopin's family moved to Warsaw shortly after his birth in 1810 when his father, a Frenchman, began teaching at the city's Lyceum, housed in the **Kazimierz Palace** (Pałac Kazimierzowski; Krakowskie Przedmieście 26/28, Śródmieście Północne; Ⓜ Nowy Świat-Uniwersytet). His first concert, aged eight, was given in what is now the Presidential Palace (p63) on 24 February 1818. From then on and during his teenage years Chopin was regularly playing on the organs of churches close to his home, including the **Visitationist Church** (Kościół Wizytek; www.wizytki.waw.pl; Krakowskie Przedmieście 34; Ⓠ Hotel Bristol).

From 1827 to 1830 Chopin lived in an annex of the **Czapski Palace** (Pałac Czapskich; Krakowskie Przedmieście 5, Śródmieście Północne; Ⓜ Nowy Świat-Uniwersytet). He played a concert at the Teatr Wielki (p78) in October 1830 before leaving Warsaw forever on 2 November. After Chopin's death in Paris in 1849 his eldest sister, Ludwika Jędrzejewicz, complied with his request to remove his heart before his body was buried. She smuggled the heart, preserved in a jar of alcohol, back to Warsaw where it was interred in a pillar of the Church of the Holy Cross (p63).

★ Top Tips

○ Limited visitation is allowed each hour; book in advance online, by phone or at the booking office at ul Tamka 43.

○ At the booking office you can also reserve a place for the free piano concerts performed by talented young musicians in the museum at 6pm on most Thursdays between January and June.

○ Download the free Chopin in Warsaw and Selfie With Chopin apps (http://en.chopin.warsawtour.pl) to locate the 15 public benches scattered across Warsaw that play a snippet of Chopin at the touch of a button.

✕ Take a Break

One of Warsaw's top coffee shops, Stor (p75), is a short stroll downhill from the museum.

Top Sight 📷
Palace of Culture & Science

This socialist realist palace, a 'gift of friendship' from the Soviet Union, has dominated central Warsaw since 1955. At 237m, it remains one of the city's tallest buildings. Take in the view from the 30th-floor observation terrace then head to ground level to enjoy the complex's many amenities including three theatres, a multiplex cinema and cool bars and cafes.

◎ MAP P64, C5

Plac Defilad 1

PKiN, Pałac Kultury i Nauki

www.pkin.pl

observation deck adult/ concession 20/15zł

⊘ observation deck 10am-8pm

Ⓜ Centrum

Stalin's Gift

Built to a design by Lev Rudniev that had been pioneered in Moscow's series of grand Stalinist-era skyscrapers, PKiN (as its full Polish name is abbreviated) was as much an ideological statement as it was architecturally symbolic. Among the uncomplimentary names Varsovians gave to the 3288-room complex was the 'Elephant in Lacy Underwear', a reference both to the building's size and the sculptures that frill the parapets and terraces. More recently, though, PKiN has become accepted and even embraced as a city icon.

Observatory & Other Attractions

PKiN remains at heart a recreation and educational facility. The top attraction is the **observation terrace**, which provides panoramic views of the city. Bring warm layers as it can be chilly outdoors here at 114m. There is also a cafe.

There are three theatres in the complex: **Teatr Dramatyczny** (☏ 22 656 6844; www.teatrdramatyczny.pl; tickets 40-90zł; 🛜) presents a mixed repertoire of shows ranging from contemporary Polish to Shakespeare and hit musicals (some with English subtitles) in its grand main auditorium and studio space; **Studio Teatrgaleria** (☏ 22 656 6941; https://teatrstudio.pl; tickets from 35zł; ⌚ gallery 11am-7pm Tue-Sun) stages more avant-garde plays and performances and has an art gallery; **Teatre Lalka** (☏ 22 656 6956; www.teatrlalka.pl; tickets from 38zł; 🚼) is devoted to puppet theatre.

Elsewhere in this vast building is **Kinoteka** (☏ 22 551 7070; www.kinoteka.pl; tickets from 25zł), one of the city's most popular multiscreen cinemas.

★ Top Tips

○ To see some of PKiN's grand interior architecture, join the guided 'Palace in a Nutshell' tour organised by **Creatours** (http://creatours.pl; adult/concession 30/25zł; ⌚ 11am-4pm), whose booth is next to the ticket office for the observation terrace.

○ The huge Congress Hall, seating 3000 and which for years hosted the Communist Party meetings as well as rock concerts, is closed for renovation.

○ Between May and August, in front of the palace's main eastern entrance, events such as film screenings and concerts are mounted – see www.placdefilad.org for details.

✖ Take a Break

Off the main lobby of the Teatr Dramatyczny, **Cafe Kulturalna** (www.kulturalna.pl; ⌚ noon-midnight; 🛜) has a buzzing atmosphere and is one of the best spots in PKiN for a drink or a casual meal.

MADE WINF TROS /SOOO /GETTY IMAGES ©

Walking Tour 🥾

Along Krakowskie Przedmieście

This wide boulevard, running from Castle Sq to ul Nowy Świat, marks the start of the so-called Royal Way and makes a great walk. The boulevard is lined with evocative churches, monuments to two key figures in Polish cultural life, landmarks associated with Chopin and wonderful examples of historic architecture.

Walk Facts

Start Stare Miasto bus and tram stop

End Nowy Świat-Uniwersytet metro station

Length 1km; one hour

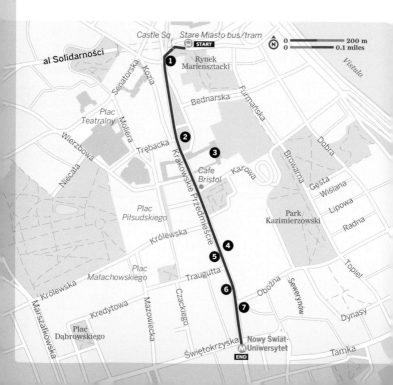

❶ St Anne's Church

Arguably Warsaw's most ornate church, **St Anne's** (Kościół Św Anny; www.swanna.waw.pl; 9am-3pm Mon-Sat, 10am-7pm Sun) sports an original trompe l'oeil ceiling, a rococo high altar and a gorgeous organ, on which a 30-minute concert is played at noon between mid-April and mid-October, except for Sundays and holidays.

❷ Monument to Adam Mickiewicz

This neoclassical **monument** (Pomnik Adama Mickiewicza) to Poland's great Romantic poet Adam Mickiewicz (1798–1855) was unveiled on the 100th anniversary of his birth. Mickiewicz is the author of the national epic poem *Pan Tadeusz*.

❸ Presidential Palace

At the age of eight, Chopin is said to have given his first public performance in what is now Poland's **Presidential Palace** (Pałac Prezydencki; www.president.pl). The entrance is guarded by four stone lions and an equestrian statue of Prince Józef Poniatowski.

❹ Warsaw University

The main entrance to **Warsaw University** (Uniwersytet Warszawski; www.uw.edu.pl) is marked by a decorative gate topped with the Polish eagle.

❺ Fibak Collection Gallery

Wojciech Fibak's superb private collection of Polish modern and contemporary art is on show at this small but packed **gallery** (Galeria Fibak; www.galeriafibak.com.pl; admission free; 11am-7pm Mon-Fri, to 5pm Sat). Among the prominent artists in the collection are Wojciech Fangor, Stefan Gierowski and Jan Lebenstein.

❻ Church of the Holy Cross

Step inside this **church** (Kościół św Krzyża; www.swkrzyz.pl; admission free; 10-11am & 1-4pm Mon-Sat, 2-4pm Sun) to view its fine baroque altarpieces and to pay homage at the second pillar on the left side of the nave. Adorned with an epitaph to Frédéric Chopin, the pillar enshrines a jar that contains the composer's heart.

❼ Monument to Nicolaus Copernicus

Standing in front of the Staszic Palace, which houses the Polish Academy of Sciences, is this 1830 bronze **monument** (Pomnik Mikołaja Kopernika) to the great astronomer Mikołaj Kopernik (1473–1543). Better known outside Poland as Nicolaus Copernicus, he proved conclusively that the earth revolves around the sun.

Andersa

Krasiński Gardens

Młodowa

Podwale

1

Długa

al Solidarności

Kozia

Ratusz Arsenal

25

Bielańska

Museum of Caricature **14**

2 Jewish Historical Institute

Senatorska

Moliera

al Solidarności

Andersa

6 **24**
Vodka Museum

Wierzbowa

40

47

21

Museum of the John Paul II Collection **11**

Senatorska

Tomb of the Unknown Soldier

Krakowskie Przedmieście

2

Elektoralna

Saxon Garden

4

10

Zachęta – National Gallery of Art

3

39 Ptasia

Hala Gwardii

Plac Małachowskiego **8**

Traugutta

Hala Mirowska

Królewska

45

13

Mazowiecka

Czackiego

36

al Jana Pawła II

Kredytowa

Ethnographic Museum

Grzybowska

12
Nożyk Synagogue

32

Plac Grzybowski

Próżna

16

Zielna

Plac Dąbrowskiego

15 Menora Info Punkt

Świętokrzyska

19 Świętokrzyska

Jasna

Plac Powstańców Warszawy Warecka

Twarda

Marszałkowska

Świętokrzyska

41

Sienkiewicza

Górskiego

38

Złota

Szpitalna

26

48

Zgoda

Plac Defilad

ZODIAK Warsaw Pavilion of Architecture

ul Chmielna

5

28

Palace of Culture & Science

31

Smolna

9

Centrum

Sienna

Emilii Plater

Złota

al Jerozolimskie

50

Złota

Chmielna

6

Warszawa Centralna Train Station

Warszawa Śródmieście Train Station

Poznańska

Nowogrodzka

Marszałkowska

Żurawia

A B C D

For reviews see

◉ Top Sights p58
◉ Sights p66
✕ Eating p71
🍷 Drinking p74
★ Entertainment p78
🛍 Shopping p79

0 — 500 m
0 — 0.25 miles

Vistula

Bednarska

Wybrzeże Kościuszkowskie

Warsaw University Library

Powidoki
Museum on the Vistula

7
5
1
3
Copernicus Science Centre

Heavens of Copernicus Planetarium

Most Świętokrzyski

23

Browarna

20
42

Dobra

BarKa
Plac Zabaw nad Wisłą

Krakowskie Przedmieście

37

Zajączka

Tamka

M Centrum Nauki Kopernik

Oboźna
Sewerynów

Dynasy

Topiel

Dobra

Solec

Nowy Świat-Uniwersytet
M

Tamka
29

Kruczkowskiego

Ordynacka

Okólnik

Fryderyk Chopin Museum

49

44
Kopernika

33
22
34
27
46

Nowy Świat

Foksal

43
al Jerozolimskie

Solec

35

18

Smolna

Warszawa Powiśle Train Station

Kruczkowskiego

Ludna

30
17

Bracka

Plac Trzech Krzyży

Książęca

Maszyńskiego

Rozbrat

Okrąg

Wilanowska

Czerniakowska

Krucza

Wspólna

Hoża

Mokotowska

Wielska

Prusa

Sights

Copernicus Science Centre

MUSEUM

1 ◎ MAP P64, G2

The fully interactive, push-the-buttons-and-see-what-happens Copernicus Science Centre pulls off that tricky feat of being both hugely fun and educational. With over a million visitors a year it is also incredibly popular: advance booking of tickets is highly recommended or you may find yourself waiting all day for a slot to enter. Check the website for exact opening times as they vary throughout the year.

Most exhibits are suited for kids 12 to 18 years old, though there's plenty on hand to amuse younger – and older – visitors. Usually on the last Thursday of the month the centre is an over-18s-only zone for its Lates events (35zł, 7pm to 10pm) with DJs and expert panels. (Centrum Nauki Kopernik; ✆22 596 4100; www.kopernik.org.pl; ul Wybrzeże Kościuszkowskie 20, Powiśle; adult/concession Mon-Fri 31/21zł, Sat & Sun 33/22zł; ⊗9am-6pm Mon-Fri, 10am-7pm Sat & Sun, usually closed 1st Mon of month; Ⓜ Centrum Nauki Kopernik)

Jewish Historical Institute

MUSEUM

2 ◎ MAP P64, B2

Just behind a blue skyscraper (which stands on the location of the Great Synagogue destroyed by the Germans), JHI houses a library and exhibitions related to Jewish culture. The building, which opened in 1928, was the place where those involved in compiling the Ringelblum Archive (p71) conducted their activities – the exhibition on this precious collection of direct testimonies about the extermination of Polish Jewry is imaginatively conceived and very moving. (JHI; Żydowski Instytut Historyczny; ✆22 827 9221; www.jhi.pl; ul Tłomackie 3/5, Śródmieście Północne; adult/concession 12/7zł, Sun free; ⊗9am-6pm Mon-Fri, 10am-5pm Sun; Ⓜ Ratusz Arsenał)

Heavens of Copernicus Planetarium

PLANETARIUM

3 ◎ MAP P64, G2

You may well find yourself wanting to make multiple visits to this far-from-average planetarium. A packed repertoire of films is projected across a 16m-wide spherical screen with headphones providing commentary in a variety of languages. Some screenings are in 3D, for which there's a slightly higher ticket price, as is the case for other events including regular laser shows and the classical music, jazz and kids' music shows. (Niebo Kopernika; ✆22 596 4100; www.niebokopernika.pl; ul Wybrzeże Kościuszkowskie 20, Powiśle; adult/concession from 22/16zł; ⊗9am-6.30pm Mon-Thu, until 9.30pm Fri, 10am-8.30pm Sat & Sun; Ⓜ Centrum Nauki Kopernik)

Tomb of the Unknown Soldier

MONUMENT

4 💿 MAP P64, D3

Dedicated to the unknown soldiers who have given their lives for Poland, this military memorial occupies the last remnant of the Saxon Palace that stood here until it was destroyed by the Germans in WWII. In a marching ceremony across the square, the pair of soldiers who guard the eternal flame are changed every hour on the hour. (Grób Nieznanego Żołnierza; Plac Piłsudskiego 1-3, Śródmieście Północne; 🚊Zachęta)

Warsaw University Library

LIBRARY

5 💿 MAP P64, F2

The stunning copper-clad building that houses the university library was awarded top prize by the Association of Polish Architects in 2000. The main facade, curving down ul Dobra, is lined with 7m-high book-shaped slabs, decorated with classical texts in the Sanskrit, Hebrew, Arabic, Greek, Russian Cyrillic and Latin alphabets.

To the rear of the building is the university **garden** (Ogród Biblioteki Uniwersyteckiej; admission free; ⏰8am-8pm), with a ground-level section open year-round and the 2000-sq-metre rooftop garden

Tomb of the Unknown Soldier

RUSLAN LYTVYN/SHUTTERSTOCK ©

open April to October. Step inside the main entrance corridor to view the interior decoration that includes classic Polish posters, originals and copies of which you can buy from **Galeria Plakatu Polskiego w BUW, Warszawa** (Polish Poster Gallery; ☏503 341 328; https://polishpostergallery.com; ☉12.30-7pm Mon-Fri, to 5pm Sat). (Biblioteka Uniwersytecka w Warszawie; ☏22 552 5178; www.buw.uw.edu.pl; ul Dobra 56/66, Powiśle; ☉8am-10pm Mon-Fri, 9am-9pm Sat, 3-8pm Sun (shorter hours in Jul & Aug); Ⓜ Centrum Nauki Kopernik)

Vodka Museum MUSEUM

6 ◉ MAP P64, C2

This small but attractive museum, hiding in a courtyard off the street, comprises mostly glass cases displaying a beautiful collection of old vodka bottles and glasses, as well as labels, advertising posters and the like. A self-guided tour (audio guide 7zł) provides a comprehensive history of Polish vodka, and can be followed by a tasting of three vodkas (you'll pay extra for premium and super-premium brand tastings). (Muzeum Wódki; ☏22 657 8996; www.muzeumwodki.pl; ul Wierzbowa 11, Śródmieście Północne; with/without vodka tasting 39/19zł; ☉11am-6pm Tue-Thu, 1-9pm Fri & Sat, noon-7pm Sun; Ⓜ Ratusz Arsenał)

Museum on the Vistula MUSEUM

7 ◉ MAP P64, F2

Poland's largest painting, measuring 1600 sq metres, by Sławomir Pawszak, covers the exterior of a pavilion designed by Austrian architect Adolf Krischanitz. Until the Museum of Modern Art in Warsaw gets its permanent home, the pavilion is being used for regularly changing exhibitions. (Muzeum nad Wisłą; ☏22 596 4010; https://artmuseum.pl; ul Wybrzeże Kościuszkowskie 22, Powiśle; adult/concession 5/2zł; ☉noon-8pm Tue-Thu, to 10pm Fri, 11am-8pm Sat, 11am-6pm Sun; Ⓜ Centrum Nauki Kopernik)

Zachęta – National Gallery of Art GALLERY

8 ◉ MAP P64, D3

Specialising in contemporary art, Zachęta organises a variety of temporary exhibitions, which change roughly every three months. A visit to this elegant neo-Renaissance building that celebrated its centenary in 2000 could include shows by Polish as well as Argentinian and Iraqi Kurdish artists in mediums ranging from painting to video installations and photography. (Zachęta – Narodowa Galeria Sztuki; ☏22 556 9651; https://zacheta.art.pl; Plac Stanisława Małachowskiego 3, Śródmieście Północne; adult/concession 15/10zł; free Thu; ☉noon-8pm Tue-Sun; 🚊 Zachęta)

Saxon Garden

ZODIAK Warsaw Pavilion of Architecture

ARCHITECTURE

9 💿 MAP P64, D5

Occupying a revamped 1960s building on which hangs a wonderful retro neon sign, this exhibition and information space promotes aspects of Warsaw's built environment past and present. *Kosmos,* the new mosaic designed by Magdalena Łapińska-Rozenbaum that covers the stairwell, is a homage to an old mosaic that originally covered the terrace wall of the pavilion. (☑ 510 205 984; http://pawilonzodiak.pl; Pasaż Stefana Wiecheckiego 4, Śródmieście Północne; admission free; ⏲11am-8pm; Ⓜ Centrum)

Saxon Garden

GARDENS

10 💿 MAP P64, C3

Covering 15.5 hectares, this splendid garden, founded in the late 17th century, became Warsaw's first public park in 1727. Initially modelled on Versailles, but later relandscaped in the more natural English style, the garden is filled with chestnut trees and baroque statues (allegories of the Virtues, the Sciences and the Elements). There's also an ornamental lake overlooked by a 19th-century water tower in the form of a circular Greek temple. (Ogród Saski; http://zielona.um.warszawa.pl; ul Marszałkowska & ul Królewska, Śródmieście Północne; 🚊 Królewska)

Museum of the John Paul II Collection   MUSEUM

11 ◉ MAP P64, B2

This impressive art collection was donated to the Catholic Church by the Carrol-Porczyński family and includes works by Rembrandt, Velásquez, Constable, Rubens, Goya, Renoir and many other famous names. Sadly, the paintings are not particularly well labelled or lit, but you'll often have the place all to yourself. Enter from ul Elektoralna. (Muzeum Kolekcji im Jana Pawła II; ☏22 620 2725; http://mkjp2.pl; Plac Bankowy 1, Śródmieście Północne; adult/concession 20/15zł; ☺10am-4pm Tue-Sun; Ⓜ Ratusz Arsenał)

Nożyk Synagogue   SYNAGOGUE

12 ◉ MAP P64, B4

The only synagogue in Warsaw to survive WWII was built between 1898 and 1902 in neo-Romanesque style. Its handsomely restored interior features grand metal chandeliers and tall vaulted colonnades. Men should cover their heads on entering. (Synagoga Nożyków; ☏22 620 4324; www.warszawa.jewish.org.pl; ul Twarda 6, Śródmieście Północne; 10zł; ☺9am-5pm Sun-Thu, to 4pm Fri; Ⓜ Świętokrzyska)

Ethnographic Museum   MUSEUM

13 ◉ MAP P64, D3

Although it's a little complicated to navigate and could do with a bit more in the way of English signage, this museum has a fine assembly of Polish folk arts and crafts, as well as fascinating temporary exhibitions. Ask at reception for directions to the traditional costumes gallery, which is a museum highlight. (Państwowe Muzeum Etnograficzne w Warszawie; ☏22 827 7641; http://ethnomuseum.pl; ul Kredytowa 1, Śródmieście Północne; adult/concession permanent exhibitions 12/6zł, Thu free, temporary exhibitions 20/10zł; ☺10am-5pm Tue, Thu & Fri, 11am-7pm Wed, 10am-6pm Sat, noon-5pm Sun; Ⓜ Świętokrzyska)

Museum of Caricature   MUSEUM

14 ◉ MAP P64, D2

A refreshing break from history museums and churches, this quirky museum holds 25,000 original works by Polish and foreign caricaturists dating from the 18th century onwards, plus satirical and humorous books, magazines and the like. Displays are rotated on a regular basis. (Muzeum Karykatury; ☏22 827 8895; www.muzeumkarykatury.pl; ul Kozia 11, Śródmieście Północne; adult/concession 9/5zł, Tue free; ☺10am-6pm Tue-Sun; 🚌 Stare Miasto)

Menora Info Punkt   COOKING

15 ◉ MAP P64, B4

Inside Charlotte Menora, this information office can advise on all aspects of Jewish Warsaw. A couple of times a month it also organises Jewish cooking classes – places can be booked via the website of POLIN (p86). Culinary tours of Poland are also run in

The Ringelblum Archive

Inscribed on Unesco's Memory of the World Register, the Ringelblum Archive is a precious collection of around 6000 documents that provide direct testimony about the extermination of Polish Jewry during WWII. It is named after the historian Emanuel Ringelblum (1900–44) who created the organisation Oneg Shabbat in November 1940 to gather documentary evidence of what was happening to Jews under German occupation.

Members of Oneg Shabbat (which means 'Joy of the Sabbath' in Hebrew) met secretly, usually on Saturday, at the building that today houses the Jewish Historical Institute (p66). The archive, which includes essays, diaries, drawings, photographs and posters, was secured in metal boxes and milk cans and buried in batches. The collection of material stopped in January 1943 in the final months of the Warsaw ghetto. In September 1946 the first part of the archive was unearthed, but it wouldn't be until December 1950 that another part of it was found by chance. Part of it still remains buried.

The archive has been digitised and preserved at the Jewish Historical Institute, where you can view a remarkable exhibition about the project. More information on the archive can be found at https://onegszabat.org.

conjunction with the Taube Center for the Renewal of Jewish Life in Poland (www.taubephilanthropies. org). (☏22 415 7926; www.polin. pl/pl/menora; Plac Grzybowski 2, Śródmieście Północne; courses from 200zł; ⏱10am-5pm Mon-Fri; ⓂŚwiętokrzyska)

Eating

Odette

DESSERTS $

16 ⓧ MAP P64, B4

Superb-quality patisserie, including mirror-glazed mousse cakes, is what grabs the eye in this lovely, contemporary-styled tearoom with leafy wallpaper. There are scores of teas to choose from including many seasonal blends. (☏604 745 444; https://odette.pl; ul Twarda 2/4, Śródmieście Północne; cakes 15zł; ⏱1-8pm Mon, 10am-8pm Tue-Sun; ⓂŚwiętokrzyska)

Charlotte Menora

BAKERY $

This second Warsaw branch of the fine bakery-cafe Charlotte (see 15 ⊙ Map p64, B4) has a Jewish lilt to its menu, taking inspiration from its location in the former Jewish heartland of the city. (☏668 669 137; http://bistrocharlotte.pl; Plac Grzybowski 2, Śródmieście Północne; mains 10-19zł; ⏱7am-midnight

Street Art around Nowy Świat

Fashionable ul Nowy Świat (New World St) is lined with restaurants, shops and cafes. Most of the buildings date from after WWII, but the restoration was so complete that the predominant style of architecture is 19th-century neoclassical.

Around the street's southern end are several pieces of public art worth taking a moment to locate. The first doesn't appear to be art at all but a stout palm growing out of the centre of the De Gaulle roundabout. With a trunk of steel and polyethylene fronds, *Greetings from Jerusalem,* created by Joanna Rajkowska and unveiled in 2002, has become a beloved city landmark.

On the side of a building, next to the bookshop Empik, look up to find one of Warsaw's most striking communist-era mosaics. Sometimes referred to as a 'girl with a gun' and designed by Władysław Zych, this 1964 piece commemorates attacks by the People's Guard communist partisans on the German-occupied building here during WWII.

Mon-Thu, to 1am Fri, 8am-1am Sat, 8am-10pm Sun; Ⓜ Świętokrzyska)

JCC Warszawa
BREAKFAST **$**

17 MAP P64, E5

The Jewish Community Centre is a welcoming, contemporary and far from strictly orthodox place that offers a variety of classes and activities, including yoga and Hebrew courses. It's most popular, however, on Sunday, when serving its excellent buffet – a vegan, kosher brunch with made-to-order shakshuka eggs.

During the rest of the week it serves hot and soft drinks only. (☑ 533 072 790; www.jccwarszawa.pl; ul Chmielna 9a, Śródmieście Północne; Sun brunch 25zł; ⏱ 11am-9pm Mon-Thu, to 4pm Fri, 10am-6pm Sun; ☎; ☒ Foksal)

Cô Tú
ASIAN **$**

18 MAP P64, E5

The wok at this simple Asian diner never rests as hungry Poles can't get enough of the excellent dishes coming from the kitchen. The menu is enormous, covering all the main bases (seafood, vegetable, beef, chicken, pork), and you'll never have to wait more than 10 minutes for your food. (☑ 22 826 8339; Pavillion 21, ul Nowy Świat 22/28a, Śródmieście Północne; mains 15-23zł; ⏱ 11am-9pm Mon-Fri, from noon Sat, noon-7pm Sun; ☒ Foksal)

Warszawska
POLISH **$$**

19 MAP P64, D4

Occupying two basement levels of Hotel Warszawa, the design of this fabulous restaurant and bar conjures up the sleek lair of a James

Bond villain. Chef Darek Baranski prepares a very tasty selection of small plates that you can mix and match to create the perfect meal. You can't go wrong with a selection of charcuterie from the house-cured meats. (📞 532 745 367; https://warszawa.hotel.com.pl; Plac Powstańców Warszawy 9, Śródmieście Północne; mains 15-71zł; ⏱7am-11pm; Ⓜ Świętokrzyska)

SAM Powiśle
CAFE $$

20 ✗ MAP P64, F3

A large communal table dominates this slick bakery, deli and cafe that aims to use organic produce from local farmers and suppliers in its dishes. It's very popular for break-fast or lunch – make sure you book early in the week for a slot at the weekend or you may find yourself waiting in line for a while. (📞 600 806 084; www.sam.info.pl/; ul Lipowa 7a, Powiśle; mains 29-39zł; ⏱8am-10pm Mon-Fri, from 9am Sat & Sun; ✍; Ⓜ Centrum Nauki Kopernik)

Cafe Bristol
CAFE $$

21 ✗ MAP P64, D2

Exemplifying the grand style of European cafe society since 1901, this is an elegant location for a posh breakfast or a light meal to set up a day's sightseeing, as well as a delightful pit stop for coffee with an expertly executed pastry or cake. (📞 22 551 1828; www.cafebristol.pl; Krakowskie Przedmieście 42/44, Śródmieście Północne; break-fast from 27zł, mains 35-43zł; ⏱8am-8pm; 📶; 🏨 Hotel Bristol)

Dawne Smaki
POLISH $$

22 ✗ MAP P64, E4

An excellent restaurant to try Polish specialities, such as herring in cream, stuffed cabbage rolls, pierogi (dumplings) and all the rest. The interior is traditional white walls, wood and lace, without being overly hokey. Try the good-value lunch specials. (📞 22 465 8320; http://dawnesmaki.pl; ul Nowy Świat 49, Śródmieście Północne; mains 35-69zł; ⏱noon-midnight Mon-Thu, to 1am Fri & Sat, to 11pm Sun; 📶)

Bez Gwiazdek
POLISH $$$

23 ✗ MAP P64, E2

'Without Stars' is a supremely successful expression of contem-porary Polish cooking. Each month chef Robert Trzópek takes inspira-tion from a different province of Poland for his set menus, which include four to six courses and can be enjoyed with wine pairings. For creative, beautifully presented dishes in a relaxed environment, this restaurant cannot be beat. (📞 22 628 0445; www.facebook.com/bezgwiazdek; ul Wiślana 8, Powiśle; set menus 100-180zł; ⏱6pm-midnight Tue-Sat, 1-4pm Sun; 📶; Ⓜ Centrum Nauki Kopernik)

Elixir by Dom Wódki
POLISH $$$

24 ✗ MAP P64, C2

Every dish at this stylish restaurant comes with a suggested pairing of Polish vodka, honey mead or a local liqueur. It's an inspired way to enjoy classics such as beef tartare and roasted duck, all of which are beautifully presented. (☎22 828 2211; www.domwodki.pl/elixir.html; ul Wierzbowa 9/11, Śródmieście Północne; mains 49-67zł; ☺noon-midnight; Ⓜ Ratusz Arsenał)

Senses Restaurant POLISH $$$

25 🍴 MAP P64, C2

Andrea Camastra's creative approach to Polish cooking has earned Senses a Michelin star. He practises molecular gastronomy and deconstruction, so don't expect a goulash, for example, to look or taste exactly like the traditional version of the dish. Not everything we sampled worked, but when it did the flavours and presentation were impressive and refreshing. (☎22 331 9697; www.sensesrestaurant.pl; ul Bielańska 12, Śródmieście Północne; set menus 320-550zł; ☺6-9.45pm Mon-Sat; 🛜; Ⓜ Ratusz Arsenał)

Drinking

E Wedel CAFE

26 🍺 MAP P64, D5

The Austrian Wedel family set up their first Warsaw chocolate factory in this handsome building in 1865. Varsovians have been flocking here for the luscious hot chocolate and sweet treats ever since. The classic drink is the one without sugar and milk (15zł). There is also plenty available to eat including savoury dishes – it's

a good breakfast choice. (☎22 827 2916; www.wedelpijalnie.pl; Szpitalna 8, Śródmieście Północne; ☺8am-10pm Mon-Fri, from 9am Sat, 9am-9pm Sun; Ⓜ Centrum)

PiwPaw Beer Heaven CRAFT BEER

27 🍺 MAP P64, E5

We'll leave it up to you how many merry evenings you spend here working your way through the nearly 80 on-tap beers, plus over a hundred more bottled ones. Suffice to say this is a superior craft-beer pub, where seemingly every bit of wall is covered in mosaics made from bottle tops. (☎534 734 945; www.piwpaw.pl; ul Foksal 16, Śródmieście Północne; ☺noon-11pm Sun-Tue, to 1am Wed & Thu, to 3am Fri & Sat; 🛜; 🚇 Foksal)

BarStudio BAR

28 🍺 MAP P64, C5

Hit the dance floor at Warsaw's most entertaining venue, doubling as the lobby bar and cafe of Studio Teatrgaleria. Depending on the DJs, you could be bopping along to a disco version of 'Anarchy in the UK' or to video images from *The Big Lebowski* and then segueing from a Disney-theme tune sing-along to rocking out to 'Highway to Hell'. (☎603 300 835; www.barstudio.pl; Plac Defilad 1, Śródmieście Północne; ☺10.30am-1am Sun & Mon, to 2am Tue-Thu, to 5am Fri & Sat; 🛜; Ⓜ Świętokrzyska)

Floating restaurant on the Vistula

Stor

COFFEE

29 🚇 MAP P64, F4

One of Warsaw's best third-wave coffee havens, Stor drips with potted-plant greenery and has appealing bakes and snacks to go with its drinks. Browse a copy of the *Coffee Spots Polska* guidebook that's published by the cafe's owner and is on sale here. (📞22 290 5190; www.stor.cafe; ul Tamka 33, Powiśle; ⏰8.30am-9.30pm; Ⓜ Nowy Świat-Uniwersytet)

Cosmo

COCKTAIL BAR

Not only is Cosmo (see 16 ❌ Map p64, B4) one of Warsaw's most sophisticated and creative cocktail bars, it is also one that aims for sustainability with a minimal-waste policy. Straws and napkins are biodegradable, and used citrus is turned into syrups and cordials to flavour drinks. The menu changes seasonally and the waiters will talk you through the delicious options. (www.cosmobar. pl; ul Twarda 4, Śródmieście Północne; ⏰5pm-midnight Mon-Wed, to 1am Fri & Sat; Ⓜ Świętokrzyska)

Między Nami

BAR

30 🚇 MAP P64, E5

'Between Us' attracts a trendy set with its designer furniture, cool art hanging on whitewashed walls, excellent drinks list and supremely friendly vibe. (📞22 828 5417; www. miedzynamicafe.com; ul Bracka 20, Śródmieście Północne; ⏰10am-11pm Mon-Thu, to midnight Fri & Sat, 2-11pm Sun; 📶; Ⓜ Centrum)

Smolna

CLUB

31 MAP P64, D5

Unless you look hip and cool, you can expect to be turned away from Warsaw's coolest club. This doesn't stop locals lining up for the all-night techno and electronic music events that take place at this historic tenement building with two dance floors, a chill-out room, three bars and a patio. (www.smolna38.com; ul Smolna 38, Śródmieście Północne; admission 30-40zł; ⏰11pm-8am Fri & Sat; 🚋Muzeum Narodowe)

Miłość

CLUB

32 MAP P64, C4

Meaning 'love', Miłość is an all-day cafe-bar that comes into its own on Friday and Saturday nights when it morphs into a club space. The two-level interior has a wall of greenery behind the DJ. In winter a tent covers the connected outdoor patio space. (📞22 657 2183; http://kredytowa9.pl; ul Kredytowa 9, Śródmieście Północne; admission 20zł Fri & Sat; ⏰noon-10pm Mon-Thu, to 5am Fri & Sat; Ⓜ Świętokrzyska)

Wrzenie Świata

CAFE

33 MAP P64, E4

This peaceful and arty bookshop and coffee house draws journalists and those interested in Polish and world affairs. It's located on a quiet backstreet behind ul Nowy Świat. (📞22 828 4998; http://wrzenie. pl; ul Gałczyńskiego 7, Śródmieście Północne; ⏰9am-10pm, from 10am Sat & Sun; 🛜; Ⓜ Nowy Świat-Uniwersytet)

A Blikle

CAFE

34 MAP P64, E5

The mere fact that A Blikle has survived two world wars and the challenges of communism makes it a household name locally. But what makes this legendary cafe truly famous is its rose jam doughnuts, for which people have been queuing up for generations. (📞669 609 706; www.blikle.pl; ul Nowy Świat 33, Śródmieście Północne; ⏰9am-10pm; 🛜; 🚋Foksal)

Warszawa Powiśle

CAFE

35 MAP P64, G5

It's all about the architecture at this cafe-bar, which occupies the spaceship-like roofed rotunda that was once one of the adjacent train station's ticket offices. In the warmer months, customers spill outside onto deck chairs and watch the skateboarders do their jumps and flips in the street-art-covered skate park beneath the raised tracks. (📞22 474 4084; www. facebook.com/warszawapowisle; Leona Kruczkowskiego 3b, Powiśle; ⏰9am-10pm Mon-Fri, from 10am Sat & Sun; Ⓜ Centrum Nauki Kopernik, 🚋Warszawa Powiśle)

Enklawa

CLUB

36 MAP P64, D4

Blue and purple light illuminates this space, with comfy plush seating, mirrored ceilings, two bars and plenty of room to dance. Check out the extensive drinks menu, hit the dance floor or observe the action from a stool on the upper balcony. Wednesday night is 'old school' night, with music from the 1970s to the '90s. Smart dress code. (📞22 827 3151; www.enklawa.com; ul Mazowiecka 12, Śródmieście Północne; ⏰10pm-3am Tue, to 4am Wed-Sat; Ⓜ Świętokrzyska)

Kafka

CAFE

37 🟢 MAP P64, F3

This pleasant cafe serving healthy cakes, quiches and sweet and savoury pancakes is a great choice. Its walls are lined with a selection of secondhand books, there are low couches to relax on, board games to play and outdoor seating overlooking the hillside Park

Kazimierzowski. (📞22 826 0822; www.kawiarnia-kafka.pl; ul Oboźna 3, Powiśle; ⏰9am-10pm; 🛜; Ⓜ Nowy Świat-Uniwersytet)

Metropolis

GAY & LESBIAN

38 🟢 MAP P64, D5

The most popular weekly gay dance night in town brings in the punters with its hunky topless staff and glam drag queens. (📞576 000 845; www.facebook.com/metropoliswarszawa; ul Sienkiewicza 7, Śródmieście Północne; admission 10zł; ⏰11pm-5am Fri & Sat; 🛜; Ⓜ Świętokrzyska)

Galeria

GAY & LESBIAN

39 🟢 MAP P64, A3

Long-running and popular late-night gay nightclub, offering

Warszawa Powiśle

KPZFOTO/ALAMY STOCK PHOTO ©

Party by the Vistula

Running for around 5km along the west bank of the river between the Poniatowski and Gdańsk bridges, the **Vistulan Boulevards** (Bulwary Wiślane; Powiśle; [M]Centrum Nauki Kopernik) have been brilliantly landscaped and designed to become an attractive riverside promenade with terraces, pavilions, public art, artificial beaches and plenty of spots to eat, drink or just watch the world go by. Popular seasonal options include **BarKa** (Map p64, G3; www.facebook.com/planbarka; Skwer im Tadeusza Kahla, Powiśle; ⏰11am-2am Sun-Thu, to 6am Fri & Sat Apr-Sep; [M]Centrum Nauki Kopernik), on a floating pontoon, and **Plac Zabaw nad Wisłą** (Map p64, G3; www.facebook.com/placzabawnadwisla; Wybrzeże Kościuszkowskie, Powiśle; ⏰Mar-Nov; [M]Centrum Nauki Kopernik), where live concerts and other events are held. Open year-round is **Powidoki** (Map p64, F2; www.facebook.com/powidoki.bistro; Wybrzeże Kościuszkowskie 22, Powiśle; ⏰noon-9pm Tue-Thu, to 3am Fri, 11am-3am Sat, 11am-8pm Sun; [M]Centrum Nauki Kopernik), which has an enviable terrace with a view across the river.

midweek karaoke and DJs at the weekend. Show up late if you want to dance and mingle with the crowd. (www.clubgaleria.pl; Plac Mirowski 1, Śródmieście Północne; admission free, Sat 10zł; ⏰9pm-5am Tue-Sun; 🚉Hala Mirowski)

Entertainment

Teatr Wielki
OPERA

40 ⭐ MAP P64, C2

Dating from 1833, destroyed in WWII and rebuilt to Antonio Corazzi's original design in 1965, this magnificent building is home to the Polish National Opera and Ballet companies. The principal 1768-seat Moniuszko Auditorium, one of the world's largest opera stages, is used for a quality repertoire of classic and new works by

Polish and international composers. (National Opera; 📞22 826 5019; www.teatrwielki.pl; Plac Teatralny 1, Śródmieście Północne; tickets 60-260zł; ⏰box office 9am-7pm Mon-Fri, from 11am Sat & Sun; [M]Ratusz Arsenał)

Filharmonia Narodowa
CLASSICAL MUSIC

41 ⭐ MAP P64, D4

Home of the world-famous National Philharmonic Orchestra and Choir of Poland, the National Philharmonic was founded in 1901. Destroyed during WWII, it was rebuilt in 1955 to house a concert hall (enter from ul Sienkiewicza 10) and a chamber-music hall (enter from ul Moniuszki 5), both of which stage regular concerts. (National Philharmonic; 📞22 551

7130; www.filharmonia.pl; ul Jasna 5,
Śródmieście Północne; tickets from
60zł; ⏱box office 10am-2pm & 3-7pm
Mon-Sat; Ⓜ Świętokrzyska)

Shopping

Chrum.com
FASHION & ACCESSORIES

42 🔒 MAP P64, F3

Leonardo's *Lady with a Piglet*?
Just one of the cheeky, quirky and
colourful print T-shirts and other
fashion accessories stocked by
this porcine-loving brand that is
constantly coming up with new
designs. The T-shirts are hand-
printed and made from good-
quality Polish cotton. (📞22 415
5224; www.chrum.com; ul Dobra 53,
Powiśle; ⏱11am-7pm Mon-Fri, noon-
6pm Sat; Ⓜ Centrum Nauki Kopernik)

Acephala
FASHION & ACCESSORIES

43 🔒 MAP P64, G4

With collections inspired by
women's-rights campaigners
and the likes of French avant-
garde photographer and writer
Claude Cahun, Monika Kędziora's
designs certainly stand out from
the crowd. The brand's flagship
concept store also stocks mens-
wear from Amsterdam-based
Delikatessen, eyewear by Sirène,
accessories and indie style mags
and books. (📞661 772 666; https://
acephalafashion.com/acs; al 3 Maja 14,
Powiśle; 🚋Warszawa Powiśle)

DecoDialogue
ARTS & CRAFTS

44 🔒 MAP P64, E4

Specialising in homewares by
Polish craftspeople, DecoDialogue

Hala Mirowska (p89)

VIDALGO/SHUTTERSTOCK ©

Market Halls

Despite much of its main hall having been converted into a modern supermarket, Hala Mirowska (p89) is worth visiting for its architecture alone. The ornate red-brick pavilion of this late-19th-century marketplace is in exceptional condition. Surrounding the main hall are traditional stalls selling fresh flowers, fruit, vegetables and other produce.

Next door is the art nouveau **Hala Gwardi** (Map p64, A3; https://halagwardii.pl; Plac Żelaznej Bramy 1, Śródmieście Północne; mains 15-25zł; ⏰9am-1am Fri & Sat, 10am-11pm Sun; 🚊Hala Mirowska) offering both food and souvenir stalls plus street-food-style outlets, bars and coffee spots. It's very relaxed with a youthful edge and something for everyone – from freshly baked pizza to sushi and craft beer. After WWII the hall was used as a bus depot, then later hosted boxing matches – hence the blown-up black and white photos that hang from the walls.

has enthusiastic staff who are delighted to chat about their carefully selected range of ceramics, linens, glass, furniture and other decorative objects. (📞510 133 163; https://decodialogue.pl; ul Kopernika 8/18, Śródmieście Północne; ⏰11am-7pm Mon-Fri, to 4pm Sat; Ⓜ Nowy Świat-Uniwersytet)

Porcelanowa
CERAMICS

45 🔒 MAP P64, C3

At this gallery you can admire and buy ceramics by some of Poland's leading contemporary potters and artists. Items include gorgeous hand-painted vases by Malwina Konopacka (http://malwinakonopacka.com) and tea sets by Marek Cecuła (https://modus

design.com). (📞501 569 444; http://porcelanowa.com; ul Kredytowa 2, Śródmieście Północne; ⏰11am-7pm Mon-Fri, to 3pm Sat; 🚊Królewska)

Cepelia
ARTS & CRAFTS

46 🔒 MAP P64, E5

Established in 1949, Cepelia is dedicated to promoting Polish arts and crafts, stocking its shops with woodwork, pottery, sculpture, fabrics, embroidery, lace, paintings and traditional costumes. The selection at this branch is particularly impressive. (📞22 827 0987; www.cepelia.pl; ul Chmielna 8, Śródmieście Północne; ⏰11am-8pm Mon-Fri, to 2pm Sat; 🚊Foksal)

Galeria Art
ART

47 MAP P64, D2

Owned by the Association of Polish Artists and Designers, this excellent gallery sells a broad range of original contemporary Polish art by its members, as well as postcards and books. (22 828 5170; www.galeriaart.pl; ul Krakowskie Przedmieście 17, Śródmieście Północne; 11.30am-7pm Mon-Fri, to 5pm Sat; Hotel Bristol)

TFH Concept
FASHION & ACCESSORIES

48 MAP P64, D5

If you're looking for contemporary streetwear courtesy of young Polish designers, you've come to the right place. Clothes and accessories feature upstairs in this attractive boutique, while downstairs you can browse retro items. (502 488 348; www.tfhkoncept.com; ul Szpitalna 8, Śródmieście Północne; 11am-8pm Mon-Sat, noon-6pm Sun; Centrum)

Marta Ruta Hats
HATS

49 MAP P64, G4

English-speaking Marta can custom-make you a lovely new hat for between 500zł to 600zł in a couple of days. Materials include felt, straw, fake fur and tweeds. She also stocks chunky handmade knit hats. (501 087 002; www.facebook.com/MartaRutaHats; ul Solec 97, Powiśle; 11am-6pm Mon-Fri; Centrum Nauki Kopernik)

Złote Tarasy
MALL

50 MAP P64, B6

The popular 'Golden Terraces' mall hosts major local and international chains, including Zara, H&M, Sephora and the Empik book and CD store. It also has many places to eat and a multiplex cinema. (22 222 2200; www.zlotetarasy.pl; ul Złota 59, Śródmieście Północne; 9am-10pm Mon-Sat, to 9pm Sun; Centrum, Warszawa Centralna)

Explore

Muranów, Mirów & Powązki

These two residential and largely uncommercial districts are where the Germans created the Warsaw Ghetto in 1940. Today the area is characterised by communist-era apartment buildings, but scattered remnants of Jewish Warsaw survive. West of Muranów lies the historic cemetery Powązki and the city's main Jewish Cemetery – both contain beautiful examples of tombstone art.

The Short List

○ **POLIN Museum of the History of Polish Jews (p86)** Learning about Poland's Jewish population past and present.

○ **Warsaw Rising Museum (p84)** Listening to first-hand accounts, and seeing filmed footage of the doomed 1944 uprising.

○ **Jewish Cemetery (p91)** Shedding tears over the incredibly moving Monument to the Children of the Ghetto.

○ **Powązki Cemetery (p91)** Navigating the avenues of grand funerary monuments.

○ **Railway Museum (p91)** Jumping on and off retro engines and carriages at this former main train station.

Getting There & Around

Ⓜ Line M1 stops at Ratusz Arsenał and Dworzec Gdański. Line M2 stops at Rondo ONZ and Rondo Daszyńskiego.

🚊 Trams 17, 33 and 41 run along al Jana Pawła II, 4, 15, 18 and 35 along ul Andersa.

Muranów, Mirów & Powązki Map on p90

POLIN Museum of the History of Polish Jews (p86)
Juliusz Klosowski/Shutterstock © Architect: Rainer Mahlamäki

Top Sight 📷
Warsaw Rising Museum

This exceptional museum, housed in a former tram power station and its surrounding grounds, traces the history of the city's heroic but doomed uprising against the German occupation in 1944 via five levels of interactive displays, photographs, film archives and personal accounts. It's an immersive, overwhelming experience that takes the majority of a day to see to do it justice.

◎ **MAP P90, B5**

www.1944.pl

adult/concession 25/20zł, Sun free

🕐 8am-6pm Mon, Wed & Fri, to 8pm Thu, 10am-6pm Sat & Sun

Ⓜ Rondo Daszyńskiego, 🚊 Muzeum Powstania Warszawskiego

Museum Exhibits

The ground floor begins with the division of Poland between Nazi Germany and the Soviet Union in 1939 and moves through the major events of WWII. An elevator (lift) then takes you to the Mezzanine (2nd floor) and the start of the uprising in 1944 with day-by-day displays.

The largest exhibit, a life-size reproduction of the B-24J Liberator heavy bomber that was used to drop supplies for insurgents, fills much of the ground-floor Liberator Hall (pictured). Here you can also watch newsreel films shot during the uprising, as well as a six-minute 3D film that recreates the view from a flight over the city in 1945 – you'll be stunned to see how much of Warsaw was destroyed.

Don't miss the basement where you can see the exhibition on Germans in Warsaw and crawl through a replica of the sewer (thankfully devoid of sewage!) and take the elevator up to the top of the building's 32m tower for a panoramic view of the city.

Freedom Park

There's still more to see outside the museum in the surrounding Freedom Park. Here stands the 156m Wall of Remembrance, inscribed with the names of 11,488 insurgents. In a niche in the wall hangs the 230kg Monter bell dedicated to Gen Antoni Chruście, commander of the Warsaw Rising armed forces and whose code name was 'Monter'. The bell is rung every 1 August on the anniversary of the outbreak of the uprising.

On the other side of the Wall of Remembrance, the *Colour of Freedom* exhibit of colourised photos of insurgents sandwiches a Rose Garden and the Art Wall gallery of contemporary artworks created by top Polish artists and inspired by the 1944 Rising and Warsaw.

★ Top Tips

○ Good days to visit the museum are Sunday (when it's free) and Monday (many other city museums are closed on Mondays).

○ In summer Freedom Park hosts music concerts, games for children and various events related to the commemoration of the anniversary of the Warsaw Rising, which is on 1 August.

○ A great online resource including movies of how pre-WWII Warsaw looked is Warsaw Rising 1944 (www.warsawrising.eu).

✗ Take a Break

The museum's 1st floor has a self-service cafe with outdoor seating on a terrace.

Across the road from the museum, drop by Wabu (p96) for a lunch of sushi and other Japanese cuisine.

Top Sight

POLIN Museum of the History of Polish Jews

Housed in one of Warsaw's best examples of contemporary architecture, this award-winning museum documents 1000 years of Jewish history in Poland. The multimedia permanent exhibition includes accounts of the earliest Jewish traders in the region through waves of mass migration, progress and pogroms, all the way to WWII, the destruction of Europe's largest Jewish community and the present-day situation.

⊙ MAP P90, C2

www.polin.pl

adult/concession main exhibition 25/15zł, temporary exhibition 12/8zł, free Thu

🕙 10am-6pm Mon, Thu & Fri, to 8pm Wed, Sat & Sun

Ⓜ Ratusz Arsenał,
🚌 Muranów or Anielewicza

Core Exhibition

Practically all aspects of local Jewish culture and history are covered from the art installation Forest (about the legendary origins of Jews in Poland) to the Postwar Years (1944 to the present).

Multimedia displays bring highlights of the story to life, such as the touchscreen about the Statute of Kalisz, the 13th-century charter that gave Jews permission to settle and follow their religion. Here you'll also see the museum's oldest object – a coin minted in Poland in the early 1200s inscribed with Hebrew letters.

A highlight is a reconstruction of the polychromatic painted ceiling and *bimah* (raised central platform for reading the Torah) of the synagogue that once stood in Gwoździec (now part of Ukraine). You can also listen to the 'Jewish Caruso' cantor Gershon Sirota, who sang in the now-destroyed Great Synagogue that once stood near Warsaw's City Hall.

Heading towards the section on the Holocaust (1939–45), the design becomes darker and more claustrophobic until you find yourself in the ghetto itself. The exhibition wraps up with multiple videos of local Jews talking about their contemporary lives.

Architecture

The museum's stunning contemporary building was designed by Finnish architectural firm Lahdelma & Mahlamäk to harmonise with the nearby Ghetto Heroes Monument. Nevertheless the architecture is otherworldly and ethereal thanks to its outsized entrance – a symbolic crack in the facade – and glass panels inscribed with Hebrew and Latin letters that read 'Polin'. This refers to the legend of the first Jews to arrive on Polish land. Fleeing persecution the refugees heard the word 'polin' (which means 'rest here') in a forest and knew they had found a place to settle.

★ Top Tips

o There's a lot to see, so set aside half a day if you plan to do all the exhibitions justice.

o All exhibitions are free on Thursday.

o Guided tours (adult/concession from 35/25zł) cover the whole exhibition or specific galleries.

o An audio guide (10zł) is available in several languages to provide even more background detail.

o Check the website for details of the temporary exhibitions and many events that regularly happen here, including film screenings, concerts and seminars.

✖ Take a Break

POLIN's self-serve cafe **Besamim** offers Jewish-style dishes with plenty of vegetarian options.

Fat White (p97) is a good spot for a decent cup of coffee – plus a haircut at the adjacent hipster barbers.

Walking Tour 🚶

Jewish Warsaw

This walk traces a route through Warsaw's former Jewish heartland, a location that is inseparable from the infamous ghetto that corralled some 400,000 Jews between 1940 and 1943. Muranów was rebuilt during the 1950s following modernist architectural principles but fragments of the ghetto remain preserved.

Walk Facts

Start Umschlagplatz
End Nożyk Synagogue
Length 3km; three to four hours

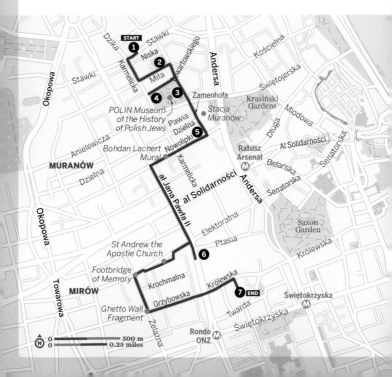

❶ Umschlagplatz

Umschlagplatz was the location of the railway terminus from which over 300,000 Jews were transported by the German military to the Treblinka extermination camp between 1942 and '43. The rectangular monument's marble walls are carved with more than 3000 forenames of the victims.

❷ Anielewicz Bunker

Also known as Miła 18, this memorial mound and **obelisk** (Bunkier Anielewicza) mark what was once a hidden shelter during the time of the Warsaw Ghetto, used by ŻOB, a Jewish resistance group. The Germans discovered it in 1943; Mordechaj Anielewicz, the leader of the Warsaw Ghetto Uprising, and several others chose to commit suicide here rather than surrender.

❸ Ghetto Heroes Monument

Nathan Rapoport's sculpted Ghetto Heroes Monument was erected in 1948 when all around still lay in ruins. Look closely and you see there are actually two monuments here – the less obvious one is the circular tablet on the ground resembling a manhole and installed in 1946. Behind it, stands the award-winning POLIN Museum of the History of Polish Jews.

❹ Willy Brandt Monument

On 7 December 1970 German chancellor Willy Brandt famously fell to his knees in front of the Ghetto Heroes Monument in a gesture of contrition for Germany's crimes against Polish Jews. This red-brick clad **memorial** (Skwer Willy'ego Brandta) commemorates that event in a corner of the park that is now named after Brandt.

❺ Esperanto Mural

Nearby, the community-arts group Stacja Muranów has commissioned several murals on the sides of buildings and courtyard arches to commemorate the area's most famous personalities, including Dr Ludovic Lazarus Zamenhof, inventor of Esperanto

❻ Hala Mirowska

Either walk or catch a tram for a couple of blocks south along al Jana Pawła II. Get off at the elegant 19th-century market hall **Hala Mirowska** (⊘most stalls 6am-6pm Mon-Sat).

❼ Nożyk Synagogue

Continue south along Jana Pawła II and turn left on ul Twarda, to find the historic and functioning Nożyk Synagogue (p70), triumphant proof of the Jewish community's survival against impossible odds.

Muranów, Mirów & Powązki

A

B

C

D

1

Powazkowska

Burakowska

17

25

Słomińskiego

Warszawa
Gdańska Train
Station

Dworzec
Gdański

Andersa

Słomińskiego

Zakroczymska

Konwiktorska

3
Powązki
Cemetery

12

al Jana Pawła II

Dzika

Stawki
Niska

Miła

Lewartowskiego

Zamenhofa

11

18

20

13

Walowa

Bonifraterska

Kościelna

Krasiński
Palace &
Garden

4

2

Okopowa

Smocza

Esperanto

POLIN Museum of
the History of
Polish Jews

Anielewicza

Dzielna

Nowolipki

Karmelicka

Stacja
Muranów

Andersa

Długa

Polish Your
Cooking

10

Jewish
Cemetery
1

Anielewicza

Pawia

Dzielna

19

MURANÓW

8
Pawiak
Prison
Museum

26

Nowolipie

22

23

Ratusz-
Arsenał

Plac
Bankowy

Senatorska

3

24

Nowolipki

Wolność

al Solidarności

Marszałkowska

Żytnia

Żelazna

Archeology of
Photography
Foundation

Elektoralna

Ptasia

Footbridge
of Memory

6

7

St Andrew
the Apostle
Church

Królewska

4

Chłodna

16 21

14

Chłodna

al Jana Pawła II

For reviews see

◉	Top Sights	p84
◉	Sights	p91
✕	Eating	p95
✕	Drinking	p96
✿	Entertainment	p98
🔒	Shopping	p99

Wolska

Warsaw
Rising
Museum

Towarowa

Grzybowska

Ghetto Wall
Fragment

MIRÓW

Twarda

Świętokrzyska

Rondo ONZ

15

Warsaw
Spire

5

Rondo
Daszyńskiego

Prosta

Pańska

Sienna

Warsaw
Ghetto
Museum

Śliska

Twarda

Żelazna

Warszawa
Centralna
Train Station

5

Grzybowska

Karolkowa

Kasprzaka

Prosta

Szarych
Szeregów

Srebrna

Chmielna

Varso
Tower

Chałubińskiego

Brylowska

Przyokopowa

Kolejowa

2
Railway
Museum

al Jerozolimskie

6

Warszawa
Zachodnia
Train Station

9
Pinball
Station

Kolejowa

al Jerozolimskie

Warszawa
Ochota
Train Station

Plac
Zawiszy

0 —————— 500 m
0 —————— 0.25 miles

Sights

Jewish Cemetery
CEMETERY

1 MAP P90, A3

Founded in 1806, Warsaw's main Jewish Cemetery covering 33.4 hectares contains more than 150,000 tombstones, the largest and most beautiful collection of its kind in Europe. Incredibly, it suffered little during WWII. A notice near the entrance lists the graves of many eminent Polish Jews, including Ludwik Zamenhof, creator of the international artificial language Esperanto. Men should cover their heads with a hat or a cap while in the cemetery.

The tomb of **Ber Sonnenberg** (1764–1822) is one of Europe's finest funerary monuments; take the first paved path on the left beyond the ticket office and when you arrive at a junction on your right, look left: it's the roofed structure over by the wall. Scattered across the cemetery and marked by black poles tipped with orange are 24 tombstones designed by noted sculptor **Abraham Ostrzega** (1889–1942), who died in Treblinka concentration camp. Look out also for the collective graves, in particular the incredibly moving **Monument to the Children of the Ghetto**, decorated with a handful of photographs of the some one million children who perished in the Holocaust; it's found to the right of the cemetery entrance besides a raised mound planted with silver birch trees. Nearby

is a bronze statue of **Dr Janusz Korczak**, director of the Jewish orphanage in Warsaw who stayed with his charges in the ghetto, despite being offered sanctuary, and accompanied them to Treblinka. A database of all who are buried here and at other Jewish cemeteries in Poland can be found at www.cemetery.jewish.org.pl. (Cmentarz Żydowski; http://warszawa.jewish.org.pl; ul Okopowa 49/51, Powązki; adult/concession 10/5zł; ⏱10am-5pm Mon-Thu, 9am-1pm Fri, to 4pm Sun; 🚋Cmentarz Żydowski)

Railway Museum
MUSEUM

2 MAP P90, B6

Occupying the former premises of Warszawa Główna, the city's main train station until the opening of Warszawa Centralna in 1975, this open-air museum is a real treat for fans of the iron way and the golden age of railways. After ogling the some 500 historical exhibits inside, including model trains, uniforms and other memorabilia, head outside to the platforms to inspect up close 50 steam, diesel and electrical engines, carriages and rolling stock. (Stacja Muzeum; 📞22 620 0480; www.stacjamuzeum.pl; ul Towarowa 3, Czyste; adult/concession 12/6zł, free Mon; ⏱10am-6pm May-Sep, 9am-5pm Oct-Apr; Ⓜ Rondo Daszyńskiego, 🚋Plac Zawiszy)

Powązki Cemetery
CEMETERY

3 MAP P90, A2

Warsaw's most prestigious cemetery covers 43 hectares and

contains the graves of well over a million souls. Illustrious Poles from all walks of life are buried here and a set of signs in Polish by the main gate lists the notables under their respective professions and areas of interest.

Here lies the grave of Nobel Prize winner for literature Władysław Reymont, the composer Stanisław Moniuszko, Chopin's piano teacher Józef Elsner and film director Krzysztof Kieślowski, among many others. The cemetery is particularly atmospheric on and immediately after **All Saints' Day** (Dzień Wszystkich Świętych; ☉1 Nov) when Varsovians visit family graves to clean them and leave wreaths, flowers and candles in coloured glass jars. The main entrance is next to St Charles

Borromeo Church. (☏22 838 5525; Powązkowska 14, Powązki; ☉7am-8pm; ☒Powązkowska)

Krasiński Palace & Garden

PALACE

4 ◉ MAP P90, D2

A meticulous replica, following its destruction by the Germans in WWII, this baroque palace was originally completed in 1683 for the nobleman Jan Dobrogost Krasiński. It now houses the National Library's special collections section. The palace is not generally open to the public but the attached garden is – it's one of the most pleasant parks in the city. Look for the contemporary *Pegasus* statues in bright colours in front of the palace on ul

Powązki Cemetery (p91)

EWG3D/GETTY IMAGES ©

Miodowa. (Pałac i Ogród Krasińskich; http://zielona.um.warszawa.pl; pl Krasińskich 5, Muranów; ⊙park 7am-midnight; Ⓜ Ratusz Arsenał)

Warsaw Spire
ARCHITECTURE

5 ◉ MAP P90, B5

The 49-storey Warsaw Spire is Poland's tallest office building and the centrepiece of a business district of shiny new tower blocks that is transforming Warsaw's former 'wild west'. At the foot of the tower is the well-designed public space Plac Europejski, home to an **Art Walk** with pods containing a free gallery of contemporary art, an ice-skating rink in winter and spaces for playing boules or splashing in fountains in the summer. (www.warsawspire.pl; plac Europejski 1, Mirów; Ⓜ Rondo Daszyńskiego)

Archeology of Photography Foundation
GALLERY

6 ◉ MAP P90, C4

Since 2008 this foundation has sought to promote Polish photography by hosting exhibitions at its gallery, publishing books and holding workshops and lectures. It also cares for the archives of 10 notable photographers, providing free access to over 60,000 images online. (Fundacja Archeologia Fotografii; ✆ 22 628 1464; http://faf.org.pl; ul Chłodna 20, Mirów; admission free; ⊙11am-7pm; ☐ Chłodna, ☐ Hala Mirowska)

St Andrew the Apostle Church
CHURCH

7 ◉ MAP P90, C4

This neo-Renaissance Catholic church, modelled on the Roman basilica of Santa Maria Maggiore, was completed in 1849 and is a survivor of WWII. The exterior is punctuated with niches containing statues of saints. (Kościół Rzymskokatolicki pw św Andrzeja Apostoła; ✆ 22 620 3747; www.parafiaandrzeja.pl; ul Chłodna 9, Mirów; ☐ Chłodna, ☐ Hala Mirowska)

Pawiak Prison Museum
MUSEUM

8 ◉ MAP P90, C3

During WWII the prison that once stood here was used by the Gestapo – that's the time period that the displays in this grimly fascinating museum focus on. Around 100,000 prisoners were held here from 1939 to 1944, of whom around 37,000 were executed. The prison was blown up by the Germans in 1944, but a mangled chunk of gateway complete with rusting, barbed wire and three detention cells (which you can visit) survive. (Muzeum Więzienia Pawiak; ✆ 22 831 9289; http://muzeum-niepodleglosci.pl; ul Dzielna 24/26, Nowolipki; adult/concession 10/5zł, free Thu; ⊙10am-5pm Wed-Sun; ☐ Anielewicza)

The Warsaw Ghetto

Nazi Germany occupied Western and Central Poland in September 1939. For the next year the Germans sealed off the city and rounded all those racially classified as Jews – as many as half a million – into a ghetto. Established in the predominantly Jewish districts of Muranów and Mirów, west of the city centre, the area was sealed off by a 3m-high brick wall in November 1040, creating the largest and most overcrowded prison in Europe. By mid-1942 as many as 100,000 people had died of starvation and epidemic diseases, even before deportation to the concentration camps had begun.

The Grossaktion Warsaw of the summer of 1942 saw over 250,000 Jews transported from the ghetto to the extermination camp at Treblinka. As news of the deaths became known, some of the remaining 50,000 people left in the ghetto decided to fight back. A small but successful resistance to further deportations in January 1943 encouraged more to join the Jewish Combat Organization (ŻOB) and Jewish Military Union (ŻZW), who began to prepare for defence. The Warsaw Ghetto Uprising began on 19 April 1943 when the Germans entered the ghetto to make a final clearing.

It was a heroic but ultimately doomed act of defiance, as block by block the ghetto was burned to the ground. Fierce fighting lasted for almost three weeks until, on 8 May, the Germans surrounded the Jewish command bunker and tossed in a gas bomb. On 16 May the Grand Synagogue was blown up. Around 13,000 Jews perished in the first urban insurgency in occupied Europe. German casualties were reported at under 150.

Metal strips along the ground and 22 wall plaques around Muranów and Mirów mark out the Ghetto's former borders and gates. The 18km of brick walls were largely demolished after WWII but fragments remain, such as at the corner of ul Żelazna and **Grzybowska** (Mur Getta Warszawskiego; Map p90, C4; 🚇 Mennica, Ⓜ Rondo ONZ). The **Footbridge of Memory** (cnr ul Chłodna & Żelazna, Mirów; 🚇 Chłodna, 🚊 Hala Mirowska) is an installation commemorating the wooden footbridge that was built in 1942 to connect the small and large ghettos. Metal poles support fibre-optic cables over the street, which at night illuminate a ghostly outline of this wartime walkway. Peer into the peepholes in the poles to see photographs of the original bridge. Set to open in 2023 is the **Warsaw Ghetto Museum** (http://1943.pl; ul Sienna 60, Mirów; Ⓜ Rondo ONZ), based in the former Bersohn and Bauman Children's Hospital, completed in 1878.

Pinball Station AMUSEMENT PARK

9 MAP P90, B6

Over 60 vintage pinball and arcade machines in full flashing and bleeping order are ready for play at this fully interactive 'museum'. Once you've paid admission you can come and go as much as you like during the day. There's also a bar. (☎ 600 633 115; https://pinball station.pl; ul Kolejowa 8a, Czyste; adult/concession 40/35zł; ⊙ 1-10pm Sun-Thu, to midnight Fri & Sat; Ⓜ Rondo Daszyńskiego)

Polish Your Cooking COOKING

10 MAP P90, D3

Come to this modern kitchen studio for English lessons in Polish cuisine, during which you'll learn to cook two classic dishes and sample several others. (☎ 501 598 681; www.polishyourcooking. com; ul Długa 44/50, Muranów; class 199zł; ⊙ 10.30am Wed & Sat, 6pm Fri; Ⓜ Ratusz Arsenał)

Eating

Gdański Bar Mleczny CAFE $

11 MAP P90, D2

A prime example of an updated 'milk bar', where wholesome budget meals were served during Poland's communist years. Gdański offers a fresh, modern interior and an English menu to choose from – line up at the hatch to place your order. (☎ 22 831 2962; www.facebook.

Stacja Muranów

Developed from a book project by writer Beata Chomątowska on the post-WWII development of Muranów, the arts and community organisation **Stacja Muranów** (Map p90, C2; ☎ 22 119 6633; http://stacjamuranow.pl; ul Andersa 13, Muranów; ⊙ 4-10pm Mon-Fri; Ⓜ Ratusz Arsenał) runs a gallery space and a cafe. It also offers walking tours (from €200 for a minimum of 10 people) of the area on a variety of themes, including the area's distinctive modernist architecture and Jewish history.

com/gdanski.bar.mleczny; ul Andersa 33, Muranów; mains 8-10zł, set meals 18-20zł; ⊙ 9am-8pm Mon-Fri, 11am-7pm Sat & Sun; 🚋 Muranowska)

Spokojna 15 PIZZA $

12 MAP P90, A2

Tucked away in a building owned by the Academy of Fine Arts and overlooking a courtyard garden, Spokojna 15 excels at thin-crust pizza but also serves other Polish and international dishes. It's a great spot for lunch if you're exploring the area. (☎ 507 782 652; http://spokojna15.com; ul Spokojna 15, Powązki; mains 19-31zł; ⊙ noon-10pm; 🚋 Powązkowska)

Kur & Wiino

CHICKEN $$

13 ❌ MAP P90, D2

The 'chicken and wine' restaurant is a contemporary rotisserie serving succulent free-range, corn-fed chickens and barbecue-sauce-basted guinea fowl. Veggies, sides, sauces and breads are all extra. The house wine, on tap at just 8zł a glass, washes it all down very nicely. (📱570 580 180; www.facebook.com/kurwino; ul Andersa 21, Muranów; whole/half/quarter chicken 38/24/16zł; 🕒noon-10pm; 🚊Muranów)

Czerwony Wieprz

POLISH $$

14 ❌ MAP P90, C4

The menu at this touristy but fun communist-era-themed restaurant, set in an outsized log cabin, is split between dishes for dignitaries such as Polish duck and those fit for the proletariat (dumplings). (The Red Hog; 📱22 850 3144; www.czerwonywieprz.pl; ul Żelazna 68, Mirów; mains 26-65zł; 🕒noon-11pm; 🚊Hala Mirowska, 🚊Chłodna)

Wabu

JAPANESE $$

15 ❌ MAP P90, B5

A wall of sake barrels greets you at Wabu, one of several swanky restaurants that face Plac Europejski. It's a sophisticated-looking place that serves reasonably good Japanese food, mainly sushi. It also has vegan options. (📱22 628 9274; www.wabu.pl; Warsaw Spire, plac Europejski 2, Mirów; sushi 13-52zł, set meals 29-217zł; 📶📲; Ⓜ️Rondo Daszyńskiego)

Winosfera

INTERNATIONAL $$$

16 ❌ MAP P90, C4

As the name suggests, there's a focus on wine at this restaurant aimed squarely at business-account holders. In an industrial-styled space with exposed brick walls, tasty, seasonally inspired dishes are presented with flair. There's a good-value lunch Monday to Friday (two/three courses 49/59zł) and a wine shop. (📱22 526 2500; http://winosfera.pl; ul Chłodna 31, Mirów; mains 67-129zł; 🕒noon-11pm Mon-Sat; 📶; 🚊Chłodna)

Drinking

Pogłos

CLUB

17 🍺 MAP P90, B1

With room for 300 revellers, a night at Pogłos might see anything from punk to reggae being played by the DJs on two different levels. It also hosts regular live music concerts by alternative and indie bands and singers. (📱504 691 435; www.facebook.com/klubpoglos; ul Burakowska 12, Powązki; tickets from 25zł; 🚊Powązkowska)

Craft Beer Muranów Piwny Świat

CRAFT BEER

18 🍺 MAP P90, D2

Work your way through 14 local craft beers, a cider and, for non-beer lovers, Prosecco – all on tap – at this cosy and convivial

pub where the friendly staff speak English. (www.facebook.com/craft beermuranow; ul Andersa 23, Muranów; ⏰3pm-midnight, to 1am Fri & Sat; 🚊Muranów)

Klubokawiarnia Jaś & Małgosia CAFE

19 🚇 MAP P90, C3

A revamp of a 1967 vintage cafe, 'Hansel & Gretel' is a pleasant spot for its range of drinks and food – its burgers are well regarded and we liked the breakfast options. It comes into its own through its variety of events including markets, film-screenings and gigs. There's outdoor seating in warmer months. (📞500 139 352; www. klubjasimalgosia.pl; al Jana Pawła II 57, Nowolipki; 🚊Anielewicza)

Fat White COFFEE

20 🚇 MAP P90, D2

Coffee lovers will be impressed by this compact, cute cafe that offers coffee prepared either by the Chemex, Aeropress or drip method, as well as the usual steam-based espresso style. It's connected to the hipster barbers Ferajna (www.ferajna.pro) in case you need a hair or beard trim. (📞570 096 017; www.facebook.com/ fatwhitecoffee; ul Andersa, Muranów; ⏰7am-8pm Mon-Fri, 8am-5pm Sat; 🛜; 🚊Muranów)

Chłodna 25 CAFE

21 🚇 MAP P90, C4

This arty, bohemian haunt has been a touchstone of the area for several years. Concerts, films,

Muranów Cinema (p98)

BERNARD BIALORUCKI/ALAMY STOCK PHOTO ©

ANOUCHKA/GETTY IMAGES ©

Arkadia

debates and lectures feature regularly in the basement space in the evenings – see its Facebook page for details. Coffee, wine, beer and homemade cakes are available all day upstairs. (506 045 827; www.facebook.com/pg/chl25; ul Chłodna 25, Mirów; 9am-11pm Mon-Fri, from 10am Sat & Sun; ; Chłodna, Hala Mirowska)

Entertainment

Warszawa Opera Kameralna

OPERA

22 MAP P90, C3

Performs a repertoire ranging from medieval mystery plays to contemporary works, but is most famous for its performances of Mozart's operas. (Warsaw Chamber Opera; 22 625 7510; www.operakameralna.pl; al Solidarności 76b, Muranów; tickets from 30zł; box office 11am-7pm Mon-Fri, 3hr before performance Sat & Sun; M Ratusz Arsenał)

Muranów Cinema

CINEMA

23 MAP P90, D3

This vintage-style cinema screens mainly art-house films in its two main halls and two smaller rooms. There's a cafe in the foyer and a shop selling DVDs. (22 635 3078; www.muranow.gutekfilm.pl; ul Andersa 1, Muranów; tickets 12-23zł; M Ratusz Arsenał)

Shopping

Ministerstwo Dobrego Mydła   HEALTH & WELLNESS

24 🔒 MAP P90, B3

The Ministry of Good Soap has gathered local fans by producing small-batch, all-vegan soaps, scrubs, oils and balms, attractively packaged and scented with natural products such as calendula and hibiscus. (📞790 772 279; www.ministerstwodobregomydla.pl; ul Dzielna 15, Nowolipki; 🚊Nowolipki)

Arkadia   MALL

25 🔒 MAP P90, B1

One of Poland's largest shopping malls, Arkadia offers some 240 shops, plus 30 cafes and restaurants and a 15-screen multiplex under one roof. (📞22 323 6767; www.arkadia.com.pl; al Jana Pawła II 82, Muranów; ⏰10am-10pm Mon-Sat, to 9pm Sun; 🚊Rondo Radosława)

Varso Tower

Completed in 2020, the 53-storey **Varso Tower** (Map p90, D5; https://varso.com; ul Chmielna 69, Mirów; 🚊Warszawa Centralna) is the centrepiece of a new office and retail development that, when it tops out at 320m, will be Warsaw's and the EU's tallest skyscraper.

Leto Gallery   ART

26 🔒 MAP P90, C3

This small gallery mainly promotes the generation of artists who came of age after the fall of communism in 1989. Exhibitions change roughly once a month. (📞661 918 814; http://leto.pl; ul Dzielna 5, Muranów; ⏰noon-7pm Tue-Fri, to 4pm Sat; 🚊Anielewicza)

Explore

Łazienki Park & Southern Śródmieście

The prime focus of this southern slice of Warsaw is lush Łazienki Park with its palaces, gardens, museums and Chopin Monument. Southern Śródmieście, earmarked by the communists for post-WWII development, is home to the city's boldest socialist realist architecture. It is also the location for some of Warsaw's best places to eat and drink.

The Short List

- **National Museum (p106)** Marvelling at Polish art and design spanning centuries.

- **Łazienki Park (p102)** Strolling through gorgeous greenery to the lovely Palace on the Isle.

- **Fotoplastikon (p110)** Looking at vintage 3D photographic images in a forerunner of a VR headset.

- **Ujazdów Castle Centre for Contemporary Art (p111)** Viewing contemporary art in a recreated 18th-century manor house.

- **Museum of Life Under Communism (p110)** Learning about all aspects of Polish life during this time.

Getting There & Around

Ⓜ Centrum and Politechnika are handy metro stations.

🚊 Lines 4, 15, 18 and 35 run along ul Marszałkowska, lines 7, 9, 2, 24 and 25 along al Jerozolimskie.

Łazienki Park & Southern Śródmieście Map on p108

Chinese Garden (p103), Łazienki Park DADFAR/GETTY IMAGES ©

Top Sight 📷
Łazienki Park

Pronounced wah-zhen-kee, this beautiful park includes manicured greens, an ornamental lake, wooded glades and strutting peacocks. Once a hunting ground, Łazienki was acquired by Poland's last monarch Stanisław August Ponia-towski in 1764 and transformed into a series of splendid gardens in which you'll find two palaces, an amphitheatre, museums and various follies.

🎯 MAP P108, F5

Park Łazienkowski

📞 504 243 783

www.lazienki-krolewskie.pl

ul Agrykola 1, Ujazdów

admission free

🕐 24hr

🚌 Plac Na Rozdrożu

The Gardens

Łazienki's 76 hectares are made up of three main types of garden: the 18th-century Italianate **Royal Garden** laid out during the time of King Stanisław August Poniatowski; the 19th-century **Romantic Garden**, which tumbles down the hill behind **Belvedere Palace** (Pałac Belwederski; ul Belwederska 52, Ujazdów; ⊋Łazienki Królewskie) and contains a number of follies; and the early-20th-century **Modernist Garden** of which the **Chopin Monument** is a focus.

Added in 2014, the **Chinese Garden** borrows from the chinoiserie style that was popular with the king and includes a pavilion and an arbour decorated with hand-glazed tiles from China and hung with red lanterns.

Palace on the Isle

Łazienki Park's centrepiece is a delightful neoclassical **palace** (Pałac na Wyspie; ☎22 506 0024; adult/concession 25/18zł, free Thu; ⊕9am-4pm Tue-Sun Oct-Apr, 10am-6pm Tue, Wed & Fri-Sun, to 8pm Thu May-Sep; ⊋Łazienki Królewskie) that stands on an island in an ornamental lake. Some 140 paintings and works of art from the king's collection are on display here. Architectural highlights include an ornate ballroom and the 17th-century marble bas reliefs depicting scenes from Ovid's *Metamorphoses* that grace the original bathhouse (*łazienki* in Polish, hence the name), which was the foundation of the palace.

★ Top Tips

o Łazienki's Facebook page (www.facebook.com/pg/Muzeum.Lazienki.Krolewskie) lists events and special exhibitions held frequently in the park.

o The park is a great location for bird spotting with scores of species nesting here year-round. The most majestic of them are the peacocks, which can often be spotted strutting around the Palace on the Isle.

✕ Take a Break

Dine on fine seasonal food, surrounded by lush greenery and flowers at **Belvedere** (☎22 558 6701; www.belvedere.com.pl; ul Agrykola 1, Ujazdów; mains 82-159zł; ⊕noon-11pm Mon-Sat, to 5pm Sun) inside the New Orangery building.

Old Orangery & Royal Theatre

The elegant **Old Orangery** (Stara Oranżeria; ☎504 243 783; adult/student 20/10zł, Thu free; ⏲9am-4pm Tue-Sun Oct-Apr, 10am-6pm Tue, Wed & Fri-Sun, to 8pm Thu May-Sep), completed in 1788, once sheltered exotic trees in the winter. It now houses a gallery featuring an impressive selection of sculpture collected from across Europe by King Stanisław August Poniatowski. The highlight is the beautifully restored Kamsetzer Colonnade, in which copies of ancient sculptures stand against background paintings of an idyllic Italian landscape.

In the same building is the **Royal Theatre** (Teatrem Królewskim; ☎22 511 5900; https://operakrolewska.pl; adult/concession 60/30zł), an 18th-century auditorium featuring beautiful stucco and trompe l'oeil decoration, which is still used for regular performances.

Myślewicki Palace & Amphitheatre

Fully renovated in 2018, the compact and semicircular-shaped **Myślewicki Palace** (Pałac Myślewicki; ☎504 243 783; adult/concession 10/5zł, free Thu; ⏲9am-4pm Tue-Sun Oct-Apr, 10am-6pm Tue, Wed & Fri-Sun, to 8pm Thu May-Sep) was designed by Domenico Merlini in 1774. The

Chopin Monument

interiors preserve the decor from the times of King Stanisław August Poniatowski, including original polychrome landscape views of Rome and Italy by Jan Bogumił Plersch.

Nearby, the mock-ruined **Amphitheatre** (Amfiteatr; www. lazienki-krolewskie.pl/en/architektura/ amfiteatr) was built in 1790 and is modelled on the Roman open-air theatre at Herculaneum, Italy. The stage, set on an islet in the lake, was once used for ballet performances for the royal court.

Museum of Hunting & Horsemanship

The **Museum of Hunting & Horsemanship** (✆ 22 522 6630; Szwoleżerów 9, Ujazdów; adult/concession 10/5zł, free Thu; ⊙9am-4pm Tue-Sun Oct-Apr, 10am-6pm Tue, Wed & Fri-Sun, to 8pm Thu May-Sep) occupies two park buildings dating from the 1820s. The **Cantonists' Barracks** features natural-history-style displays of stuffed forest animals, birds and trophy heads, alongside

Chopin Monument

Designed in 1907 by Wacław Szymanowski, this fabulous art nouveau bronze statue wasn't erected until 1926. Such was its symbolic power to Poles that it was blown up by the occupying Germans in 1940. Fortunately, the statue mould survived WWII so a copy could be resurrected in Łazienki Park in 1958.

Piano concerts of the composer's music are held beside the statue every Sunday at noon and 4pm from mid-May to September.

the antique weapons used to kill them – either fascinating or horrific depending on your views about hunting. In the **Kubicki Stables** are a dozen historical horse-drawn vehicles, including carriages and a sleigh, as well as horse equipment used on aristocratic estates.

ARTUR BOSACKI/GETTY IMAGES ©

Top Sight 📷
National Museum

Drawing on a collection of some 830,000 works of art, both local and international, this is Poland's largest museum. It will come as a revelation for anyone unfamiliar with Polish creativity through the ages. The diverse exhibits include Europe's only permanent show of medieval Nubian paintings, gems of Polish design, and superb art from the 19th to 21st centuries.

◉ MAP P108, E1

Muzeum Narodowe
www.mnw.art.pl
al Jerozolimskie 3,
Śródmieście Południowe
adult/concession 20/12zł,
Tue free
🕙10am-6pm Tue-Thu, Sat
& Sun, to 9pm Fri
🚊Muzeum Narodowe

Ground Floor

The **Faras Gallery** displays 8th- to 14th-century tempera paintings that once adorned the plaster walls of a cathedral in the medieval city of Faras in present-day Sudan. A team of Polish archaeologists helped excavate and save the remains of the cathedral in the early 1960s before the construction of the Aswan Dam flooded the area. The haunting religious images are displayed in a configuration that recalls their original placement in the cathedral.

Contrast this African religious art with the European works in the **Gallery of Medieval Art**. Key pieces include the 1390 *Grudziądz Polyptych,* the altarpiece from Pruszcz Gdański, and the incredibly contemporary-looking *Christ in Distress,* a painted wood carving from 1502.

1st- & 2nd-Floor Galleries

The small, but wonderful **Polish Design Gallery** displays fine examples across a range of products from ceramics and fabric prints, to furniture, toys and electronic devices organised chronologically from the early 20th century to current times

There's plenty to see in the **Gallery of 18th to early 20th Century Art**. The star exhibit is Room 105's *The Battle of Grunwald,* a nearly 10m-long epic canvas painted by Jan Matejko in 1878.

The **Gallery of 20th and 21st Century Art** contains an example from Wojciech Fangor's amazing *'E series'* of painted circles that pulsate with their dynamic colour ranges. A famous graphic artist, Fangor also designed the murals in the stations for Line 2 of the metro.

On the 2nd floor the **Old Masters Galleries** showcase dazzling decorative arts as well as royal regalia, including the gilt- and fur-trimmed coronation mantle of Augustus III.

★ **Top Tips**

o Permanent exhibitions are free on Tuesdays.

o The museum also mounts interesting temporary exhibitions; some free, others for a small addition to the entry fee.

o Exhibits are well labelled and free English leaflets are available in most galleries. If you need more background info, consider renting an audio guide (adult/concession 10/7zł).

o Guided tours in a range of languages can be booked Monday to Friday from 9am to 3pm or by email (edukacja@mnw.art.pl).

✖ **Take a Break**

For a drink or a light meal close to the museum, **Café Lorentz** (☑882 037 779; http://cafelorentz.pl; al Jerozolimskie 3, Śródmieście Południowe; ☺10am-6pm; ☎; ☒Muzeum Narodowe) is a good choice and has outdoor seating.

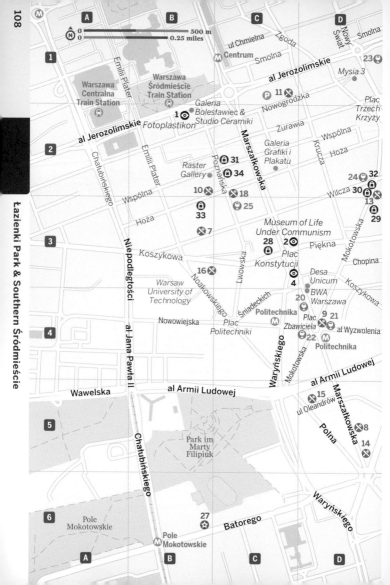

A | B | C | D

1

500 m
0.25 miles

ul Chmielna   Zgoda
Centrum
Smolna
al Jerozolimskie   Nowy Świat
Smolna

Mysia 3   23

Warszawa Centralna Train Station

Warszawa Śródmieście Train Station

Galeria Bolesławiec & Studio Ceramiki
1   Fotoplastikon

11

Nowogrodzka

Żurawia

Plac Trzech Krzyży

Emilii Plater

al Jerozolimskie

2

Chałubińskiego

Emilii Plater

Wspólna

Galeria Grafiki i Plakatu

Krucza   Hoża

Wspólna

Marszałkowska

31
34

Raster Gallery

10
33

18
25

24   32
Wilcza   30
13
29

Mokotowska

Poznańska

Hoża

7

3

Koszykowa

16

Warsaw University of Technology

Nowowiejska

Lwowska

Museum of Life Under Communism

28

Plac Konstytucji

4

Piękna

Desa Unicum

BWA Warszawa

20

Plac Politechniki

Śniadeckich

Politechnika

Plac Zbawiciela

9   21
22

Chopina

Koszykowa

Mokotowska

al Wyzwolenia

Politechnika

4

al Jana Pawła II

Niepodległości

Waryńskiego

Mokotowska

Marszałkowska

Wawelska

al Armii Ludowej

al Armii Ludowej

15
ul Oleandrów

Polna

8

14

5

Park im Marty Filipiuk

6

Pole Mokotowskie

27

Batorego

Pole Mokotowskie

Waryńskiego

A | B | C | D

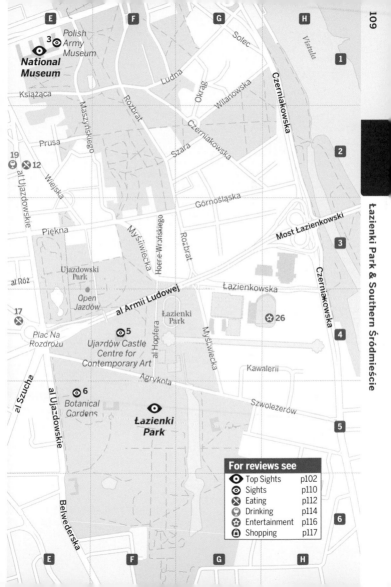

Łazienki Park & Southern Śródmieście

National Museum
3 Polish Army Museum

Solec
Vistula

Książąca
Ludna
Okrąg
Wilanowska
Czerniakowska

1

Rozbrat
Maszyńskiego
Czerniakowska

Prusa
Szara

19
12

Wiejska
Górnośląska

2

Piękna
Myśliwiecka
Most Łazienkowski

Hoene-Wrońskiego
Rozbrat

3

Ujazdowski Park
al Róż
Łazienkowska
Czerniakowska

Open Jazdów
al Armii Ludowej
Łazienki Park
26

17

Plac Na Rozdrożu
5 Ujazdów Castle Centre for Contemporary Art
al Hopfera
Myśliwiecka

al Szucha
Agrykola
Kawalerii

4

6 Botanical Gardens
Łazienki Park
Szwoleżerów

al Ujazdowskie

5

For reviews see

	Top Sights	p102
	Sights	p110
	Eating	p112
	Drinking	p114
	Entertainment	p116
	Shopping	p117

Belwederska

6

E F G H

Sights

Fotoplastikon
MUSEUM

1 🎯 MAP P108, B2

Photography enthusiasts will be thrilled by this late-19th-century contraption. Reputedly the last working example of its kind in Europe, it consists of a large rotating drum that you peer into via individual eyepieces to see stereoscopic 3D photos. The 48 images on display vary fairly often and include ones in colour. Every Sunday the set is of Warsaw in the early 20th century. (📞22 629 6078; http://fotoplastikonwarszawski.pl; al Jerozolimskie 51, Śródmieście Południowe; adult/concession 6/4zł, Thu free; ⊙10am-6pm Wed-Sun; Ⓜ Centrum)

Museum of Life Under Communism
MUSEUM

2 🎯 MAP P108, C3

This small, privately run museum, devoted to the communist period in Poland's history, has found its spiritual home situated over a KFC and overlooking socialist realist Plac Konstytucji. There's a year-by-year timeline and a focus on different aspects of the People's Republic of Poland (PRL) from politics to fashion. It's all attractively laid out and, by Warsaw standards, not too overwhelming to digest. (Muzeum Życia w PRL; 📞511 044 808; https://czarprl.pl; ul Piękna 28/34, Śródmieście Południowe; adult/concession 10/8zł; ⊙10am-6pm Mon-Thu, noon-8pm Fri, noon-6pm Sat & Sun; 🚊 Plac Konstytucji)

Polish Army Museum
MUSEUM

3 🎯 MAP P108, E1

Tracing the history of the Polish armed forces since the 10th century, this museum is one for military enthusiasts. There's not a whole lot of English explanations but most of what you can see – including weapons, armour and uniforms – is generally self-explanatory. Kids will enjoy exploring the museum grounds (free; 10am to 4pm daily), which are littered with decommissioned armaments including big guns, old tanks and fighter aircraft. (Muzeum Wojska Polskiego; 📞22 629 5271; www.muzeumwp.pl; al Jerozolimskie 3, Śródmieście Południowe; adult/concession 15/8zł, free Thu; ⊙10am-5pm Wed, to 4pm Thu-Sun; 🚊 Muzeum Narodowe)

Plac Konstytucji
SQUARE

4 🎯 MAP P108, C3

Completed in 1952, this expansive square is the centrepiece of the Marszałkowska Residential District (MDM). Although contemporary shopfronts, commercial signage and parked cars mar the socialist realist vision of the architecture, wonderful details remain, not least the heroic worker reliefs carved into facades and the giant pair of lamps at the southern end.

Return in the evening to see the animated neon **Volleyball Player**, designed by Jan Mucharski in 1960. (Śródmieście Południowe; Ⓜ Plac Konstytucji)

Ujazdów Castle Centre for Contemporary Art

ARTS CENTRE

5 MAP P108, F4

Interesting and creatively quirky arts events, including exhibitions, performance art and large-scale installations, are all staged within the Ujazdów Castle. The current building is a 1970s recreation of the castle as it was in its 18th-century guise, but there has been a fort on the bluff above the Vistula here since the 13th century. (Centrum Sztuki Współczesnej Zamek Ujazdowski; 22 628 1271; https://u-jazdowski.pl; ul Jazdów 2, Ujazdów; adult/concession from 10/5zł; Thu free; 11am-6pm Tue, Wed & Sun, noon-8pm Thu & Fri, 10am-7pm Sat; Plac Na Rozdrożu)

Botanical Gardens

GARDENS

6 MAP P108, E5

Founded in 1818, the Botanic Gardens covers 22.5 hectares in the northwest corner of Łazienki Park and contain a diverse collection of species ranging from European trees, such as the beech, to exotic specimens like the gingko biloba from China. There are also greenhouses for tropical flowers and plants that you can visit by guided tour. (Ogród Botaniczny; 22 553 0511; www.ogrod.uw.edu.pl; al Ujazdowskie 4, Ujazdów; adult/concession gardens 10/5zł, greenhouses 5zł; gardens 9am-8pm Mon-Fri, from 10am Sat & Sun Apr-Aug, 10am-6pm Sep, 10am-5pm Oct, greenhouses 10am-2pm Wed-Fri, to 5pm Sat & Sun Apr-Sep; Plac Na Rozdrożu)

Soviet Tank, Polish Army Museum

BASTICHANDREW/SHUTTERSTOCK ©

Łazienki Park & Southern Śródmieście Sights

Open Jazdów

Open Jazdów (Map p108, E4; https://jazdow.pl; ul Jazdów, Ujazdów; 🚊Plac Na Rozdrożu) is a charming wooded enclave in the heart of Warsaw. The colony of some 20-odd Finnish wooden cottages have been here since 1945 and host a variety of organisations that stage various public events throughout the year – see Open Jazdów's Facebook page for more details.

Eating

Kuchnia Konfliktu

VEGAN, VEGETARIAN $

7 🍴 MAP P108, B3

Refugees and new immigrants to Poland are given a leg up by being employed by this mainly vegan cafe, decorated with greenery. The menu chalked on the blackboard changes daily and staff should be able to translate. A three-course meal for just 30zł is brilliant value and portions are huge – so come hungry. (www.facebook.com/kuchnia konfliktu; ul Wilcza 60, Śródmieście Południowe; mains 22zł; �9 1-8pm Tue, Wed & Sat, to 10pm Thu-Sat; 🛜; 🚊Koszykowa)

Prasowy

CAFETERIA $

8 🍴 MAP P108, D5

Epitomising the best of self-serve, milk-bar culture is Prasowy with its classy twist on a retro interior and a democratic menu of hearty Polish staples. (📞666 353 776; https://prasowy.pl; ul Marszałkowska 10/16, Śródmieście Południowe; mains 6-19zł; �9 9am-8pm Mon-Fri, 11am-7pm Sat & Sun; 🖉; 🚊Plac Unii Lubelskiej)

Charlotte Chleb i Wino

FRENCH $

9 🍴 MAP P108, D4

This casual French-Polish bakery and bistro dishes up tantalising croissants and pastries at the break of dawn, then transitions to big salads and crusty sandwiches for lunch and dinner, and finally to wine on the terrace in the evening. Great value for money. (📞662 204 555; www.bistrocharlotte.pl; Plac Zbawiciela, Śródmieście Południowe; mains 10-19zł; �9 7am-midnight Mon-Thu, to 1am Fri, 8am-1am Sat, 8am-10pm Sun; 🛜; 🚊Plac Zbawiciela)

Youmiko Vegan Sushi

SUSHI $

10 🍴 MAP P108, B2

Once you've sampled Youmiko's freshly made vegan takes on sushi, including toppings made from edamame beans, sweet potato and jackfruit, you may never feel like going back to the fish version again. Put yourself in the chefs' hands and treat yourself to the degustation feast (69zł). (📞22 404 6736; www.facebook.com/youmiko.vg; ul Hoża 62, Śródmieście Południowe; sushi from 8zł, mains 25zł; �9 noon-10pm Mon-Thu, to 11pm Fri & Sat, 1-9pm Sun; 🖉; 🚊Hoża)

Bibenda

POLISH $$

11 MAP P108, C1

If this is modern Polish cooking, we love it. The beef cheeks doused in a 'magic' sticky sauce is a superb comfort dish. Or there's burnt sweet potato in a peanut sauce with a zing of lime, just one of several very good vegetarian options. The space combines a bar with a casual restaurant and feels contemporary and welcoming – no wonder it's popular. (502 770 303; www.bibenda.pl; ul Nowogrodzka 10, Śródmieście Południowe; mains 29-65zł; noon-midnight Tue-Sat, 10am-10pm Sun; ; Krucza)

Rusiko

GEORGIAN $$

12 MAP P108, E2

Consistently tapped as Warsaw's best Georgian restaurant, Rusiko serves very authentic dishes such as freshly baked cheese and egg-filled breads and creamy nutty dips, as well as wines and brandies from the region. If the restaurant is full (reservations are recommended), try the neighbouring wine bar. (22 629 0628; www.rusiko. pl; al Ujazdowskie 22, Śródmieście Południowe; mains 27-39zł; restaurant noon-11pm Tue-Sun, wine bar from 3pm Tue & Wed, to midnight Thu & Fri, noon-midnight Sat, noon-11pm Sun; Plac Trzech Krzyży)

Przegryź

EUROPEAN $$

13 MAP P108, D2

Original paintings by top Polish artist Marcin Maciejowski and colourfully patterned tiles create a warm, quirky atmosphere at this fab all-day bistro. Breakfast dishes are served until noon, after which you can choose from items like free-range chicken, beef cheeks or potato dumplings. The coffee is excellent, and there is even a menu for your pooch. (www.facebook. com/przegryz; ul Mokotowska 52, Śródmieście Południowe; mains 29-38zł; 9am-10pm Mon-Fri, from 11am Sat & Sun; ; Plac Trzech Krzyży)

Cool Cat

INTERNATIONAL $$

14 MAP P108, D5

This certainly is one cool cat, with its twisted ribbon of pink neon illuminating the bar, hipster customers and an appealing menu that trips from excellent Japanese ramen (go for the one with a chunky tentacle of octopus) to that staple of the Israeli breakfast table, shakshuka. (733 932 393; www.facebook.com/TheCoolCatTR; ul Marszałkowska 8, Śródmieście Południowe; mains 25-45zł; 9am-10pm; Plac Unii Lubelskiej)

MOD

INTERNATIONAL $$

15 MAP P108, D5

What's not to love about MOD? After slurping on its tasty ramen (including a vegan version) or laksa noodles, round off your meal with one of Warsaw's best doughnuts, freshly baked on the premises, and a classic cocktail. (570 205 746; http://moddonuts.com; ul Oleandrów 8, Śródmieście Południowe; mains 28-42zł; 10am-midnight Tue-Sat, to 10pm Sun & Mon; Politechnika)

Hala Koszyki
FOOD HALL $$

16 ⊗ MAP P108, B3

If you can't decide what you'd like to eat, or you're part of a group with diverse tastes, this artfully converted early-20th-century market hall is the answer. It's stacked with a wide variety of options from sushi and tapas bars to craft-beer stations and artisan chocolate shops. (www.koszyki. com; ul Koszykowa 63, Śródmieście Południowe; mains 10-50zł; ⊙9am-9pm Mon-Sat, to 8pm Sun; 🚇Plac Konstytucji)

Regina
CHINESE $$

17 ⊗ MAP P108, E4

Channelling a NYC Chinatown meets Little Italy groove, Regina is the kind of place where a steaming bowl of chilli beef with broccoli or General Tsoi's spicy chicken can be enjoyed alongside a pepperoni-topped pizza. It's also a cool and glamorous place for cockails with the downstairs bar illuminated by a glittering chandelier. (🕿22 621 4258; www.facebook.com/Reginako-szykowa1; ul Koszykowa 1, Śródmieście Południowe; mains 20-24zł; ⊙noon-10pm Mon, to midnight Tue-Fri, 10am-midnight Sat, 10am-10pm Sun; 🛜; 🚇Plac Na Rozdrożu)

Alewino
INTERNATIONAL $$$

A series of rustically chic rooms wrapped around a courtyard house one of Warsaw's best restaurants and wine bars (see 29 🔒 Map p108, D3). The wine selection is excellent and features some

top Polish labels. The creative cooking uses seasonal produce and includes more than the usual throwaway vegetarian option. Service is relaxed and friendly. (🕿22 628 3830; www.alewino. pl; ul Mokotowska 48, Śródmieście Południowe; mains 56-65zł; ⊙5-11pm Mon, from noon Tue-Sat; 🛜🥢; 🚇Plac Trzech Krzyży)

Kieliszki na Hożej
POLISH $$$

18 ⊗ MAP P108, C2

The availability of 160 wines by the glass is reason enough to swing by 'Glasses on Hoża', but there's also its accomplished contemporary Polish cooking to take into account. Small but perfectly formed dishes include starters such as pickled cherries and a splendid beef tartare, and mains of cloudlike cottage cheese dumplings in an umami mushroom broth. (🕿22 404 2109; http://kieliszkinahozej.pl; ul Hoża 41, Śródmieście Południowe; mains 44-89zł; ⊙noon-10pm Mon-Wed, to 11pm Thu & Fri, 2-11pm Sat; 🚇Hoża)

Drinking

Klub SPATiF
CLUB

19 ⊙ MAP P108, E2

In the mid-20th century, this club-bar in an elegant tenement building was a hang-out for Warsaw's arty and theatrical set. Revived, it has bounced back better than ever, playing host to a cool crowd who love to dance at events such as regular live concerts by the Mała Orkiestra Dancingowa, play-

PETER PTSCHELINZEW/ALAMY STOCK PHOTO ©

Hala Koszyki

ing 1930s Polish pop. (📞22 625 1498; http://klubspatif.pl; al Ujazdowskie 45, Śródmieście Południowe; admission depending on event; ⏱6.30pm-late Wed-Sat; 🚊Plac Trzech Krzyży)

Gram
BAR

20 🚇 MAP P108, D4

Play pinball and old-school arcade computer games at this cute, circus-themed bar where the beers go for a bargain 10zł. On your way up from the bigger and rowdier Warmut bar on the ground floor, admire and perhaps take a selfie against the super-cool backdrop of 3D models of Warsaw landmark buildings hanging from the ceiling. (www.facebook.com/grammarszalkowska; ul Marszałkowska 45/49, Śródmieście Południowe; ⏱4pm-1am Sun-Tue, to 2am Wed, to 3am Thu & Fri, 2pm-3am Sat; 🚊Plac Zbawiciela)

Plan B
BAR

21 🚇 MAP P108, D4

A legendary Warsaw watering hole, this grungy, upstairs bar on Plac Zbawiciela invariably draws a crowd. Find some couch space and relax to smooth beats from regular DJs. On warm summer evenings the action spills out onto the street, giving the square the feel of a summer block party. (📞503 116 154; www.planbe.pl; al Wyzwolenia 18, Śródmieście Południowe; ⏱11am-late; 🚊Plac Zbawiciela)

Coffee Karma
CAFE

22 🚇 MAP P108, D4

Laid-back Coffee Karma has an enviable perch on Plac Zbawiciela, with comfy couches and a light menu. The warmly lit interior hung with art is a fine place to work through a morning-after slump with the aid of caffeine. (📞22 875 8709; www.facebook.com/coffeekarma.warszawa; Plac Zbawiciela 3/5, Śródmieście Południowe; ⏰7.30am-10pm Mon-Fri, from 10am Sat & Sun; 🛜; 🚃Plac Zbawiciela)

Cuda na Kiju
CRAFT BEER

23 📍 MAP P108, D1

There are some 16 different draught ales on tap at this popular multi-level bar. A big draw is that its seats spill out on the huge paved courtyard within the city's former Communist Party HQ, making it one of the coolest inner-city hang-outs in warm weather. (www.facebook.com/cudanakijumultitapbar; ul Nowy Świat 6/12, Śródmieście Południowe; ⏰noon-1am Mon-Thu, to 2am Fri & Sat, to midnight Sun; 🚃Muzeum Narodowe)

Woda Ognista
COCKTAIL BAR

24 📍 MAP P108, D2

Colourful characters and auspicious events from Poland's nightlife from the 1920s and '30s inspire the seasonal cocktails at 'Fire Water'. Everything is professionally prepared by friendly bartenders who work at a handsome bar beneath a pressed-tin ceiling. (📞22 258 1441; www.wodaognista.com; ul Wilcza 8, Śródmieście Południowe;

⏰5am-midnight Sun-Thu, to 2am Fri & Sat; 🛜; 🚃Plac Trzech Krzyży)

Beirut
BAR

25 📍 MAP P108, C3

Hip and informal, this super-popular Lebanese-style drinking den bills itself as a 'hummus & music bar'. Most customers appear content to focus on the alcoholic beverages, but the creamy hummus and other Middle Eastern bites are attention worthy. It can get crowded, but DJs keep the mood bubbling along nicely. (www.facebook.com/beiruthummusbar; ul Poznańska 12, Śródmieście Południowe; mains 10-25zł; ⏰noon-2am; 🛜; 🚃Hoża)

Entertainment

Legia Warsaw
SPECTATOR SPORT

26 ⭐ MAP P108, H4

To give it its full official name, the Marshall Józef Piłsudski's Municipal Stadium is the home stadium of the city's football (soccer) team Legia Warsaw, one of the most successful in the Polish league. To buy a ticket at the box office you'll need to bring photo ID (preferably your passport). (Legia Warszawa; 📞22 318 2000; http://legia.com; ul Łazienkowska 3, Ujazdów; adult/concession from 45/35zł; ⏰box office 11am-7pm Mon-Fri, 10am-5pm Sat, 11am-3pm Sun; 🚃Legia-Stadion)

Southern Śródmieście's Art Galleries

Southern Śródmieście is a top Warsaw spot to scout out local creative work at the area's galleries. As well as the following you'll also find photography on display at the **Leica 6×7 Gallery** in **Mysia 3** (Map p108, D1; ☎603 767 574; https://mysia3.pl; ul Mysia 3; ☉10am-8pm Mon-Sat, noon-6pm Sun; 🚇Muzeum Narodowe).

Desa Unicum (Map p108, D3; ☎22 621 6669; www.desa.pl; Plac Konstytucji 2; ☉11am-7pm Mon-Fri, to 4pm Sat) Sells reprints of works by famous Polish artists and illustrators, such as Rafał Olbiński and Edward Dwurnik. Some of the images are transferred to mugs, ties and scarves, making for unusual gifts.

BWA Warszawa (Map p108, D4; www.bwawarszawa.pl; ul Marszałkowska 34/50; ☉2-6pm Wed-Sat; 🚇Plac Konstytucji) Showcases Polish contemporary artists and takes part in regular events such as Warsaw Gallery week every September.

Raster Gallery (Map p108, B2; ☎22 245 1239; www.rastergallery.com; ul Wspólna 63; ☉noon-6pm Tue-Sat; 🚇Hoża) A pioneer in promoting the Central European contemporary art scene. It hosts various events and talks as well as exhibitions, which change roughly every two months.

Galeria Grafiki i Plakatu (Map p108, C2; ☎22 621 4077; www.galeriagrafikiiplakatu.pl; ul Hoża 40; ☉11am-8pm Mon-Fri, 10am-5pm Sat; 🚇Hoża) Sells original Polish poster prints and graphic art, both originals and reproductions.

Stodoła

LIVE MUSIC

27 ⭐ MAP P108, B6

One of Warsaw's biggest and longest-running live-music stages, Stodoła is a great place to catch local and touring singers and bands. It started out in 1956 showcasing jazz but has since branched out into all genres of music and other live performances. (☎22 825 6031; www.stodola.pl; ul Batorego 10, Śródmieście Południowe; ☉box office 9am-9pm Mon-Fri, to 2pm Sat; Ⓜ Pole Mokotowskie)

Shopping

Tebe

FOOD, GIFTS & SOUVENIRS

To say that Tebe (see 1 Ⓞ Map p108, B2) sells traditional Polish gingerbread does it a disservice. The edible and decorative pieces created here by Teresa Bilska are mini works of art and make for light, portable and sweet souvenirs. Coffee is also served in gingerbread cups that you can eat afterwards. (☏ 693 528 671; www.tebe.waw.pl; al Jerozolimskie 51; ⏰ 10am-6pm Mon-Fri, to 2pm Sat; Ⓜ Centrum)

Pan tu nie stał
FASHION & ACCESSORIES

28 🔒 MAP P108, C3

Worth a visit as much for its quirky interior design as its products, this fashion brand started in Łódź in 2009. The inspiration for some of its prints on T-shirts, socks, underwear and other accessories is derived from Polish cultural products from the mid-20th century. It's a fun spot to pick up a nonstandard Polish souvenir or gift. (☏ 887 887 772; https://pantuniestal.com; ul Koszykowa 34/50, Śródmieście

Południowe; ⏰ 11am-7pm Mon-Sat; 🚋 Plac Konstytucji)

Robert Kupisz
FASHION & ACCESSORIES

29 🔒 MAP P108, D3

With a clever logo made up of both Latin and Cyrillic script, Robert Kupisz' unisex streetwear is deliberately designed to be oversized and super casual. Even so, there's an elegance to his pieces that you can check out in the showroom on the upper level of a courtyard off ul Mokotowska. (☏ 506 170 801; www.robertkupisz.com; ul Mokotowska 48/204, Śródmieście Południowe; ⏰ 11am-7pm Mon-Fri, noon-4pm Sat; 🚋 Plac Trzech Krzyży)

Legia Warszawa (p116) match

DZIUREK/SHUTTERSTOCK ©

Ania Kucsyńska
FASHION & ACCESSORIES

30 🔒 MAP P108, D2

Darling of Warsaw's fashion scene, Ania Kucsyńska crafts womens' clothes that are both elegant and sporty. Her collections are inspired by strong female role models such as Simone de Beauvoir and Peggy Guggenheim. Stylish accessories include bags in canvas and leather. (☎22 622 0276; https://aniakuczyns ka.com; ul Mokotowska 61, Śródmieście Południowe; ⏰11am-7pm Mon-Sat; 🚋Plac Trzech Krzyży)

Pracownia Pędzli i Szczotek
HOMEWARES

31 🔒 MAP P108, C2

Three generations of the Baryliński family have been making, selling and repairing brushes of all shapes and sizes from this tiny shop since 1952. (☎22 621 7656; ul Poznańska 26, Śródmieście Południowe; ⏰10.30am-5.30pm Mon-Fri, to 2pm Sat; 🚋Hoża)

Mo61 Perfume Lab
PERFUME

32 🔒 MAP P108, D2

The staff at Mo61 will help you create your own unique perfume from the bottled scents they have produced in Grasse in the south of France. It's all very elegant and cleanly designed. (☎601 652 593; http://mo61.pl; ul Mokotowska 61, Śródmieście Południowe; ⏰11am-7pm Mon-Fri, to 4pm Sat; 🚋Plac Trzech Krzyży)

KABAK
FASHION & ACCESSORIES

33 🔒 MAP P108, B3

Super-colourful Polish design socks in lots of fun patterns, plus scarves, belts and other fashion accessories, are sold by this brand whose philosophy is based on fair trade principles. (☎693 794 092; https://kabak.com.pl; ul Hoża 51, Śródmieście Południowe; ⏰10am-7pm Mon-Fri, noon-4pm Sat; 🚋Hoża)

Lniany Zaułek
HOMEWARES

Fine-quality Polish linens and towels are sold from this tiny shop (see 30 🔒 Map p108, D2). You can buy the material by the metre as well as made up into scarves or blankets. (☎22 629 6339; https://lnianyzaulek. com; ul Mokotowska 61, Śródmieście Południowe; ⏰10am-6pm Mon-Fri, to 3pm Sat; 🚋Plac Trzech Krzyży)

Pracownia Sztuki Dekoracyjnej
ARTS & CRAFTS

34 🔒 MAP P108, C2

The oldest bronze-metal foundry in Warsaw, in business since 1862. Pick up exceptional pieces in the shape of candleholders, mirror and picture frames, and wall lamps. (☎22 629 2045; www.lopienscy.pl; ul Poznańska 24, Śródmieście Południowe; ⏰8am-5pm Mon-Fri; 🚋Hoża)

Explore
Praga & Eastern Warsaw

Praga is gentrifying as creatives and entrepreneurs move into this once gritty, working-class area. This hip district offers a buzzing nightlife scene to supplement its stock of tourist sights, including interesting museums, a decent zoo, languid riverside beaches and original pre-WWII industrial architecture revamped for 21st-century leisure.

The Short List

○ **Praga Museum of Warsaw (p128)** *Learning all about the fascinating history of this east bank of the Vistula district.*

○ **Neon Museum (p122)** *Exploring the bright lights of communist-era signs.*

○ **National Stadium (p128)** *Reliving the classic moments of Euro 2012 at the impressive stadium.*

○ **Warsaw Zoological Gardens (p128)** *Being charmed by the wide array of animals that live in this historic zoo.*

○ **Polish Vodka Museum (p132)** *Tasting different styles of the local spirit at this interactive museum.*

Getting There & Around

Ⓜ Line 2 has stations at National Stadium and Dworzec Wileński.

🚋 Services 4, 13, 20, 23, 26 and 28 connect Dworzec Wileński with the Old Town. Rondo Waszyngtona is a handy tram stop close by the National Stadium.

🚆 Suburban trains stop at the National Stadium.

Praga & Eastern Warsaw Map on p126

National Stadium (p128)

NATIONAL STADIUM ARCHITECTS GMP ARCHITEKTEN ZARNELL/GETTY IMAGES ©

Top Sight 📷
Neon Museum

Plenty is packed into the Neon Museum's com-pact exhibition space with around 100 signs on display – some with their neon tubes restored and illuminated, others not. The meticulously researched and clearly presented explanation boards make a visit here more than simply about eye candy: it's a crash course in the beauty and history of this iconic artform.

◉ MAP P126, G3

Muzeum Neonów

www.neonmuzeum.org

ul Mińska 25, Kamionek

adult/concession 13/10zł

🕑 noon-5pm Mon, Tue, Thu & Fri, to 6pm Sat, 11am-5pm Sun

🚊 Bliska

About the Museum

In the early 2000s photographer Ilona Karwińska (http://ilonakarwinska.com) and her partner David Hill began a project to document the striking neon signs that were common across the Eastern Bloc. From the 1930s to the 1970s, such neon displays had illuminated prominent Warsaw buildings, but by the dawn of the 21st century many had fallen into disrepair or had been scrapped altogether. Karwińska and Hill decided to collect and conserve these signs, the first one being that of **Berlin** – a 1975-vintage sign that once hung above the Capital Textile and Clothing Enterprise in Plac Konstytucji.

Exotic-sounding, non-Polish words such as **Relax** and **Dancing** were used for these signs, which were, in their day, literally the only bright spots in a communist Warsaw devoid of commercial billboard advertising. Alternatively, dazzling neon in cursive script or bold graphics would advertise exactly what the shop sold, such as **Mydła Farby** (Soap and Paint) or **Maszyny Doszycia** (Sewing Machines).

Around Soho Factory

Once you've seen the signs in the museum take a look around the Soho Factory complex to find some more examples. Next to the museum on an office block hangs the old cinema sign **Kino Praha**. The restaurant **Warszawa Wschodnia** reuses the neon sign that once hung at the train station of the same name, while a vivid-red **coffee pot** and steaming white cup hang next to the restaurant Komu Komu. The wall of the same building is illuminated by the softly glowing golden sign **Jubliler**, measuring 8m by 4m, that once adorned a jewellery store on al Jerozolimskie, and the equally large **Emilia** from a 1960s furniture store on ul Emilii Plater.

★ **Top Tips**

○ Visit late in the day to see the neon signs on the exterior of the museum and other buildings around the Soho Factory complex in their full glowing glory.

○ Pick up Ilona Karwińska's *Neon Revolutions* coffee-table book in the gift shop, or buy your own small piece of neon art – international shipping can be arranged.

✗ **Take a Break**

Splash out on contemporary Polish cuisine in **Warszawa Wschodnia** (📞 22 870 2918; www. mateuszgessler.com. pl; Soho Factory, ul Mińska 25, Kamionek; mains 58-78zł, tasting menu 150zł; ⏱24hr; 📶; 🚋Bliska); the Monday to Friday set three-course lunch is a bargain at 25zł.

Walking Tour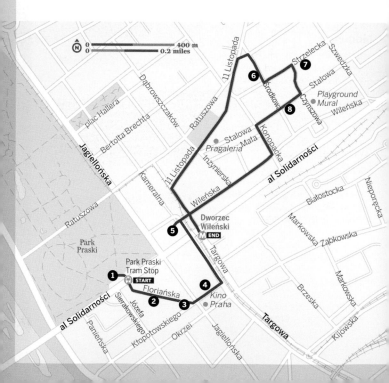

Old & New Praga

Praga rewards casual wandering and general hanging out. Stara (Old) Praga contains architectural relics of the area's past Jewish population, while Nowa (New) Praga is peppered with artists studios, galleries, vintage and antique shops, plus striking, large-scale pieces of street art.

Walk Facts

Start Park Praski tram stop

End Dworzec Wileński metro station

Length 3km; two to three hours

❶ Park Praski

Wander around Park Praski to find its *Giraffe* sculpture and to view the three bears living in the concrete pit.

❷ St Michael & St Florian Cathedral

This 1904 neo-Gothic-style **cathedral** (Katedralna Św Michała Archanioła i Św Floriana; http://katedra-floriana.waw.pl), with twin 75m spires, was destroyed in WWII and rebuilt in the early 1970s.

❸ Praga Courtyard Band Monument

This **bronze sculpture** (Pomnik Kapeli Praga) honours the five-piece bands who played in tenement courtyards before WWII. Opposite, famous figures from the world of Polish cinema are carved in stone on the façade of the **Kino Praha**.

❹ Former Mikveh

This area was once the heart of Jewish Praga – a fragment remains at the **Former Mikveh**, the bathhouse used by women for monthly ritual cleansing.

❺ St Mary Magdalene Cathedral

Warsaw's main Polish Orthodox **cathedral** (Katedra Metropolitalna pw Św Marii Magdaleny; http://katedra.org.pl) was built in 1869 to serve the growing number of Russians arriving to live in Praga. Its interior dazzles with gilded frescoes and multiple icons.

❻ Warsaw Fight Club Mural

On ul Środkowa look up to see a couple of brawling gents in 18th-century frock coats and breeches in Conor Harrington's *Warsaw Fight Club Mural*.

❼ Eastern Warsaw Mural

Spanish artist Sebas Velasco's contribution to the city's street art is this giant nightscape of a youth in a hoodie, created in 2016. Nearby is the the **Playground Mural** of a group of children playing around a globe-shaped climbing frame, by Lithuanian artist Ernest Zacharevic.

❽ Galeria Stalowa

To view art you can hang on your own walls, drop into **Galeria Stalowa** (https://stalowa.art.pl; ⊙noon-7pm Mon-Fri, to 5pm Sat) as you make your way back towards the metro station at Dworzec Wileński.

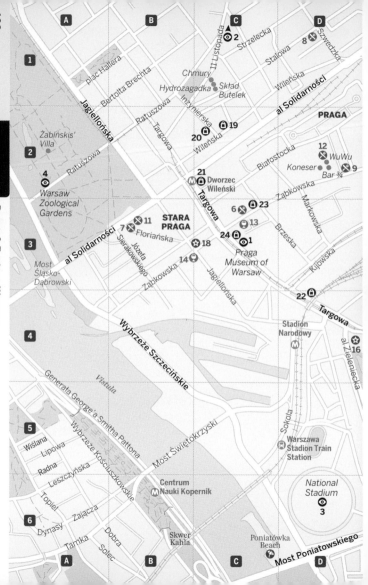

PRAGA

STARA PRAGA

Żabiński's Villa

Warsaw Zoological Gardens

Chmury

Hydrozagadka

Skład Butelek

Dworzec Wileński

Praga Museum of Warsaw

Koneser

WuWu

Bar ¾

Most Śląsko-Dąbrowski

Stadion Narodowy

Warszawa Stadion Train Station

Centrum Nauki Kopernik

National Stadium

Skwer Kahla

Poniatówka Beach

Vistula

plac Hallera

Bertolta Brechta

Jagiellońska

Ratuszowa

Ratuszowa

Targowa

Inżynierska

11 Listopada

Strzelecka

Stalowa

Szwedzka

Wileńska

al Solidarności

Białostocka

Ząbkowska

Markowska

Brzeska

Kijowska

al Solidarności

Floriańska

Józefa Sierakowskiego

Ząbkowska

Jagiellońska

Targowa

Wybrzeże Szczecińskie

Generała George'a Smitha Pattona

Wybrzeże Kościuszkowskie

Most Świętokrzyski

Wiślana

Lipowa

Radna

Leszczyńska

Topiel

Zajęcza

Dynasy

Tamka

Dobra

Solec

Sokola

Zieleniecka

Targowa

Most Poniatowskiego

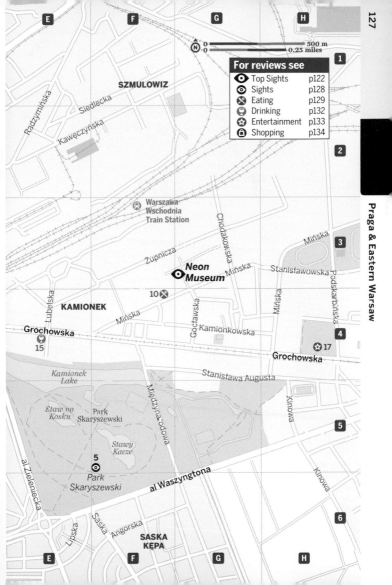

For reviews see

◉	Top Sights	p122
◉	Sights	p128
✖	Eating	p129
🍷	Drinking	p132
★	Entertainment	p133
🔒	Shopping	p134

SZMULOWIZ

Siedlecka

Radzymińska

Kawęczyńska

Warszawa Wschodnia Train Station

Żupnicza

Chodakowska

Mińska

Neon Museum

Stanisławowska

Mińska

10 ✖

Goclawska

Kamionkowska

Mińska

Podskarbińska

Lubelska

KAMIONEK

Mińska

Grochowska

15

Grochowska

★17

Stanisława Augusta

Kamionek Lake

Staw na Kosku

Park Skaryszewski

Stawy Kacze

Międzynarodowa

Kinowa

al Zieleniecka

5
◉
Park Skaryszewski

al Waszyngtona

Kinowa

Lipska

Saska

Angorska

SASKA KĘPA

Praga & Eastern Warsaw

Sights

Praga Museum of Warsaw

MUSEUM

1 ◎ MAP P126, C3

Occupying three tenement buildings spanning the 18th and 19th centuries, this museum does a fantastic job of covering Praga's rich and varied history. It includes creative displays of art, photos, memorabilia and other artefacts, art installations, restored Jewish prayer rooms and fascinating recordings of locals talking on a wide variety of topics.

A joint ticket (adult/concession 20/15zł) covers here and the main Museum of Warsaw (p40) in the Old Town. (📞22 518 3400; http://muzeumpragi.pl; ul Targowa 50/52, Stara Praga; adult/concession 10/7zł, free Thu; ⏰10am-6pm Tue, Wed & Fri-Sun, to 8pm Thu; Ⓜ️Dworzec Wileński)

Bródno Jewish Cemetery

CEMETERY

2 ◎ MAP P126, C1

Having suffered great damage during WWII and almost total destruction during Poland's communist years, this historic graveyard, where Jews have been buried since 1743, has at last gained a degree of protection and preservation. Learn about the cemetery's history and Jewish burial practices in the excellent exhibition centre located beside the gates, then walk through an avenue of silver birch trees to witness the scattered piles and fragments of some 20,000

tombstones: an unbelievably moving experience. (Cmentarz Żydowski na Bródnie; 📞22 678 7453; http://warszawa.jewish.org.pl; ul św Wincentego 15, Bródno; 10zł; ⏰10am-4pm Sun-Thu. to 2pm Fri; 🚋Rondo Żaba)

National Stadium

STADIUM

3 ◎ MAP P126, D6

This prominent landmark on the east bank of the Vistula was constructed for the Euro 2012 football championships on the site of a communist-era stadium. Its red-and-white patterning references the Polish flag, and the interior can seat 58,000 spectators for either sporting or entertainment events. Visitors can access an observation point for a view of the interior, or join a daily tour in English; check the website for times and to book tickets. (PGE Narodowy; 📞22 295 9000; www.stadionnarodowy.org.pl; al Poniatowskiego 1, Kamionek; adult/concession observation point 12/7zł, guided tours 22/15zł; ⏰9am-9pm; Ⓜ️Stadion Narodowy, 🚋Rondo Waszyngtona)

Warsaw Zoological Gardens

ZOO

4 ◎ MAP P126, A2

Established in 1928, this well-managed zoo is home to some 3000 animals representing 500 species from across the world, including bears, wolves, hippopotamuses and two male gorillas. There are even sharks and other sea creatures in what is Poland's largest aquarium. The elephant house, where there's also a cafe, is particularly impressive and the leafy grounds make for pleasant wandering throughout the year. (Miejski Ogród Zoologiczny w Warszawie; 📞 22 619 4041; https://zoo.waw.pl; ul Ratuszowa 1/3, Nowa Praga; adult/concession Oct-Mar 20/15zł, Apr-Sep 30/20zł; ⏱ 9am-6pm Apr-Sep, to 3.30pm Dec & Jan, to 4pm Feb & Nov, to 5pm Mar & Oct; 🚋 Park Praski)

Park Skaryszewski   PARK

5 ◉ MAP P126, F5

Created in 1905, this leafy and prettily landscaped 58-hectare park contains interlinked ponds and a lake, several cafes and monuments to, among others, Ignacy Jan Paderewski (1860–1941); during the interwar years the park was named after this famous Polish pianist and statesman. (al Waszyngtona; 🚋 Rondo Waszyngtona)

Eating

Coś na ZĄBkowskiej   EASTERN EUROPEAN $

6 ✖ MAP P126, C3

A log-burning stove keeps it cosy at this convivial cafe-bar where dishes include goose goulash and herring on rye bread with seaweed. It also offers a tempting range of homemade bagel sandwiches.

In 2018 the facade of Coś' 1870 building was wrapped in foil, a public artwork by Polish artist Piotr Janowski (www.piotrjanowski.net), who made his name by covering his Palm Springs home in similar silvery material. (📞 22 618 1579; www.facebook.com/cosnazabkowskiej;

Praga & Eastern Warsaw Eating

Rhinoceros, Warsaw Zoological Gardens

DANNY YE/SHUTTERSTOCK ©

Żabińskis' Villa

The incredible true life story of how zoo director Jan Żabiński and his wife Antonia helped save over 70 Jews during WWII has become famous through the book and movie *The Zookeeper's Wife*. Within Warsaw's Zoo, the elegant modernist **villa** (Willa Żabińskich; Map p126, A2; ☑603 059 758; https://zoo.waw.pl; ul Ratuszowa 1/3, Nowa Praga; zoo admission plus 5zł; ☉11am & 1pm 1st Sun of month & by appointment; 🚊Park Praski), where the Żabińskis lived and risked their lives by hiding Jews, is open for a guided tour – and it's well worth doing.

The building has been restored and redecorated much as it was during the Żabińskis' time of residence, when some of the tamer zoo animals shared what was fondly known as the 'Crazy Star Villa' with the family. Antonia was a skilled pianist and you can see her piano, on which she would play Offenbach's *La Belle Hélène* as a warning signal that Germans were approaching. Occasional concerts are still held today in the villa's living room and, during summer, in the gardens outside.

In the basement hiding place are displays about the Jews who passed through here and were saved, including the renowned sculptor Magdalena Gross, whose animal figures can be seen around the zoo gardens. In the former dining room there is also a small display from the priceless entomological collections of Dr Szymon Tenenbaum – these had been entrusted to the Żabińskis by Tenenbaum before he was relocated to the ghetto in 1941.

ul Ząbkowska 9, Stara Praga; bagel sandwiches 21-24zł; ☉noon-10pm, to 11pm Fri & Sat; Ⓜ Dworzec Wileński)

Rusałka
CAFETERIA $

7 🍴 MAP P126, B3

This retro milk bar, decked out in lime green and pine walls, attracts a devoted clientele from the nearby hospital and surrounds. It's a serve-yourself affair for staples of the Polish kitchen. (ul Floriańska 14, Stara Praga; mains 6-8zł; ☉9am-5.45pm Mon-Fri, to 4.45pm Sat, 10am-4.45pm Sun; ☑; 🚊Park Praski)

ArtBistro Stalowa 52
POLISH $$

8 🍴 MAP P126, D1

It's worth making the trip out to the edges of Praga to sample chef Dariusz Tomczyk's contemporary Polish cuisine. He uses the best seasonal produce for dishes such as pheasant broth and dumplings and beef stuffed with speck at this relaxed bistro sharing premises with an excellent boutique hotel. (☑22 252 0503; https://artbistro.pl; ul Stalowa 52, Nowa Praga; mains 39-65zł; ☉7am-10pm Mon-Fri, from 8am Sat & Sun; 🚊Szwedzka, 🚊Czynszowa)

Skamiejka
RUSSIAN $$

9 MAP P126, D2

Specialising in Russian and Georgian cuisine, Skamiejka exudes a cosy warmth with its quirky decor including samovars, matryoshka dolls and old LPs of Slavic crooners. Warm up on hearty soups, such as *ucha* (a fish broth), and fill up on plump dumplings and savoury pancakes. (☏512 123 967; www.facebook.com/Skamiejka; ul Ząbkowska 37, Szmulowizna; mains 20-25zł; ☺noon-10pm Tue-Sun; ☏; Ⓜ Dworzec Wileński)

Komu Komu
INTERNATIONAL $$

10 MAP P126, F4

The globetrotting menu at this casual and warmly decorated spot within one of Soho Factory's repurposed industrial buildings swings by Mexico via the Middle East to create crowd-pleasing tapas-style dishes along with flatbreads and falafel. It's popular for a lazy weekend breakfast or brunch.

Call ahead to book a slot in its Finnish-style **sauna** (60zł per 50 minutes for up to three people) made out of a converted shipping container that's parked in front of the restaurant. (☏508 817 766; www.facebook.com/komukomupraga; 25 ul Mińska 25, Kamionek; mains 31-49zł; ☺noon-11pm Mon-Thu, to 2am Fri, 9.30am-2am Sat, 9.30am-11pm Sun; ☺Bliska)

Le Cedre 61
LEBANESE $$

11 MAP P126, B3

Choose from a wide range of hot and cold mezze and mains at this

Bródno Sculpture Park

A project of the Museum of Modern Art, **Bródno Sculpture Park** (Park Bródnowski; https://artmuseum.pl/en/wystawy/park-rzeby-na-brodnie; Bródno; ☺Rembielińska) offers a selection of contemporary sculptures by some famous artists, including Paweł Althamer, Youssouf Dara, Olafur Eliasson and Jens Haaning. Ai Weiwei's enigmatic contribution *To Be Found* consists of the broken pieces of replica antique Chinese vases buried around the park. See the website for an interactive map of the park and details of annual events.

long-running, colourfully decorated Middle Eastern restaurant. There's a fair number of vegetarian options and a chance that you may be lucky and attend when someone has booked ahead for a performance by a belly dancer. (☏22 670 1166; www.lecedre.pl; al Solidarności 61, Stara Praga; mains 36-59zł; ☺11am-11pm; ☺; Ⓜ Dworzec Wileński, ☺Park Praski)

Zoni
POLISH $$$

12 MAP P126, D2

Chef Aleksander Baron pulls out all the stops with his contemporary take on old Polish dishes, such as Ruthenian pierogi (dried pike roe dumplings) and *zraz* (an aged beef roulade). Produce is seasonal and the presentation beautiful. The industrial chic setting, incorporating the five giant vodka stills of the old factory, is very impressive. (☎22 355 3001; https://zoni.today; pl Konesera 1, Szmulowizna; mains 68-160zł, tasting menu from 260zł; ⏲noon-11pm; 🛜; Ⓜ Dworzec Wileński)

Drinking

W Oparach Absurdu
BAR

13 Ⓔ MAP P126, C3

It's best to make a reservation if you want to be sure of getting a table at the eternally popular 'In the Fumes of Absurdity' bar. Old carpets and an eclectic bric-a-brac interior make for a cosy atmosphere, and it has a great choice of local beers, other drinks and comfort food. (☎660 780 319; www.facebook.com/woparachabsurdu; ul Ząbkowska 6, Stara Praga; ⏲noon-3am, to 5am Fri & Sat; Ⓜ)

Centrum Zarządzania Światem
LOUNGE

14 Ⓔ MAP P126, B3

If the TV series Friends were to be reset in Warsaw, Centrum could double for Central Perk. Friends do gather in comfy chairs around low tables at this cosy cafe-bar to sip coffee, drink inventive cocktails (try the bacon-laden twist on a Bloody Mary) and munch on crispy tarte flambée. (☎22 618 2197; www.centrumswiata.com; ul Stefana Okrzei 26, Stara Praga; ⏲8am-11pm Mon-Thu, to midnight Fri, 10am-midnight Sat, 10am-11pm Sun; 🛜; Ⓜ Dworzec Wileński)

Galeria Sztuki
CAFE

This cosy antique-style cafe-bar (see 23 Ⓐ Map p126, C3) is a great place to rest your feet while exploring Praga. It serves some of the best coffee in town, along with delicious

Koneser Revamped

The handsome 19th-century brick buildings that once were the **Koneser Vodka factory** (Map p126, D2; ☎22 128 4444; http://koneser.eu; Plac Konesera, Szmulowizna; Ⓜ Dworzec Wileński) are the star turn in the latest chapter in the hip revamp of industrial Praga. Here you'll find office spaces (hello Google!), the groovy hotel **Moxy**; the interactive and entertaining **vodka museum** (Muzeum Polskiej Wódki; ☎22 419 3150; https://muzeumpolskiejwodki.pl/en/; adult/concession 40/28zł; ⏲11am-8.30pm Sun-Thu, to 9.30pm Fri & Sat), where entry is by tour (those led by English-speaking guides leave 40 minutes past the hour); the fine dining restaurant Zoni (p131); several other restaurants and bars, including **Bar ¾** (☎22 419 3152; www.facebook.com/bartrzyczwarte) and **WuWu** (☎22 355 3002; https://wuwu.bar; 🛜) both of which – naturally – specialise in drinks with a vodka base; and a shopping mall with a focus on Polish products.

EDDIE GERALD/ALAMY STOCK PHOTO ©

Warszawa Wschodnia (p123)

cakes and wines by the glass, and does breakfast (mostly egg-based) until noon. (📞 22 619 8109; http://caffee.stanowski.pl; ul Ząbkowska 13, Stara Praga; ⏰ 9am-11pm Mon-Thu, to midnight Fri, from 10am Sat, to 10pm Sun; 🛜; Ⓜ Dworzec Wileński)

E Wedel
CAFE

15 🚇 MAP P126, E4

You'll immediately know where this place is from the sweet chocolatey fragrance coming from E Wedel's historic confectionary factory. Satisfy your cravings for hot chocolate by taking a seat in the cafe, based in one of a pair of 19th-century tollgates built in the neoclassical style. (Pijalnia Czekolady E Wedel; 📞 22 619 5010; www.wedelpijalnie.pl; ul Jana Zamoyskiego 36, Kamionek; ⏰ 9am-7pm Mon-Sat, 11am-6pm; 🚆 Lubelska)

Łysy Pingwin
PUB

The 'Bald Penguin' (see 23 🔒 Map p126, C3) is a classic old-school Praga bar. Hunker down with your beer or vodka shot at low tables made of wooden crates and chalk something on the blackboard walls. (📞 22 618 0256; www.facebook.com/lysypingwin; ul Ząbkowska 11, Stara Praga; ⏰ 3pm-midnight; Ⓜ Dworzec Wileński)

Entertainment

Teatr Powszechny
THEATRE

16 ⭐ MAP P126, D4

With three auditoriums of different sizes, this repertory theatre company stages an impressive range of works from both international and local playwrights. Contact them to see which shows have

Clubbing at ulica 11 Listopada 22

This cool street art–decorated courtyard is home to a trio of popular bars and live music venues. **Chmury** (Map p126, C1; ☑505 849 386; www.facebook.com/pg/kawiarniachmury; ul 11 Listopada 22, Nowa Praga; tickets from 10zł; ⏱4-11pm Sun-Thu, to 3am Fri & Sat; ⊡Inżynierska) is a homage to the TV series and movie *Twin Peaks* with an intimate performance space and bar that is a nice spot to hang out regardless of whether there's a concert on. **Hydrozagadka** (☑502 070 916; www.hydrozagadka.waw.pl; ul 11 Listopada 22, Nowa Praga; ⏱6pm-midnight, to 3am Fri & Sat; ⊡Inżynierska) has room for around 400 people and hosts indie bands and singers from all over Europe and the US, while **Skład Butelek** (☑505 849 386; www.skladbutelek.pl; ul 11 Listopada 22, Nowa Praga; ⏱6pm-midnight, to 3am Fri & Sat; ⊡Inżynierska) offers a jam session every Thursday and more live acts on other nights.

English subtitles. (☑22 818 2516; www.powszechny.com; ul Zamojskiego 20, Kamionek; tickets from 60zł; Ⓜ Stadion Narodowy, ⊡Stadion Narodowy)

Sinfonia Varsovia Orchestra
CLASSICAL MUSIC

17 ⭐ MAP P126, H4

Check online for details of the classical concerts played occasionally at this home base of the Sinfonia Varsovia Orchestra, the Polish Chamber Orchestra and a 13-piece brass ensemble. There are plans to build a new concert hall here in the future. (☑22 582 7082; www.sinfoniavarsovia.org; ul Grochowska 272, Kamionek; ⊡Praga-Południe-Ratusz)

Kino Praha
CINEMA

18 ⭐ MAP P126, C3

This three-screen cinema has a pleasant cafe and occupies a building that has a facade carved with images of famous Polish actors and directors. (☑22 343 0310; www.kinopraha.pl; ul Jagiellońska 26, Stara Praga; tickets from 21zł; Ⓜ Dworzec Wileński)

Shopping

Look Inside
VINTAGE

19 🔒 MAP P126, C2

In an area well endowed with antique and vintage stores, Look Inside stands out for its cool selection and attractive displays. It also has contemporary items including fine porcelain by Ćmielów Design Studio and works by local artists and printers. (☑668 405 284; https://lookinside.pl; ul Wileńska 21, Nowa Praga; ⏱11am-7pm Mon-Fri, noon-4pm Sat; Ⓜ Dworzec Wileński)

Cafe Melon
VINTAGE

20 🔒 MAP P126, C2

Worth searching out if you're in the market for a piece of vintage Polish glass, crystal, china and stoneware. The cafe (which serves excellent coffee) also stocks postcards and some books. (📞792 925 982; https://vintagekolektyw.pl; ul Inzynierska 1, Nowa Praga; ⊙10am-7pm Mon-Fri; Ⓜ Dworzec Wileński)

Galeria Wileńska
MALL

21 🔒 MAP P126, C2

Pretty much all your shopping needs will be met by this modern mall that includes many international fashion brands, the hyper-market Carrefour, and plenty of fast-food outlets and cafes. (📞22 331 1333; www.galeriawilenska.pl; ul Targowa 72, Stara Praga; ⊙9am-9pm Mon-Thu, to 10pm Sat, 10am-8pm Sun; Ⓜ Dworzec Wileński)

Cieszkowski
HATS

22 🔒 MAP P126, D4

This tiny workshop has been making good-quality hats for men and women since 1864. Its classic style is the Szyprówka peaked cap in black (145zł). (📞22 818 1768; ul Targowa 18, Stara Praga; ⊙10am-5.30pm Mon-Fri, to 2pm Sat; Ⓜ Stadion Narodowy)

Płyty Gramofonowe
MUSIC

23 🔒 MAP P126, C3

Mainly secondhand but also some new vinyl LPs are sold in this store, attractively decorated with retro music posters. Old jazz platters are a speciality. (📞516 518 876; https://plytygramofonowe.pl; ul Ząbkowska 11, Stara Praga; Ⓜ Dworzec Wileński)

Bazar Różyckiego
MARKET

24 🔒 MAP P126, C3

For a taste of a bygone Warsaw, take a swing through this traditional open-air market. Stroll along stalls selling voluminous ladies' underwear, frilly wedding dresses and bargain mens' suits, as well as cheap cigarettes, booze and home-made pickles in jars. (http://bazar-rozyckiego.pl; ul Targowa 54, Stara Praga; ⊙7am-5pm Mon-Fri, 8am-4pm Sat; Ⓜ Dworzec Wileński)

Walking Tour 🥾

Saska Kępa

*This delightful residential neighbourhood is
studded with architectural gems of the 1920s
and '30s. It's favoured by Warsaw's diplomatic
community whose embassies occupy some of
the modernist villas designed by architects such
as Bohdan Lachert and Józef Szanajca, who were
influenced by the likes of Le Corbusier and Walter
Gropius.*

Walk Facts

Start Rondo Waszyngtona
tram or bus stop

End Rondo Waszyngtona
tram or bus stop

Length 3km; two hours

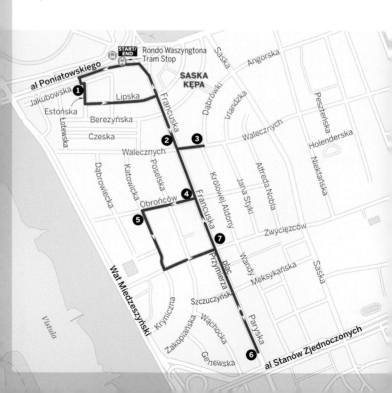

❶ Eden

Drop by **Eden** (www.facebook.com/eden.bistroo; Jakubowska 16; mains 19-35zł; ⏱10am-10pm Tue-Thu, to 11pm Fri & Sat, to 8pm Sun; 🛜), a super-cool design bistro serving creative vegan food, third-wave coffee and organic wine. It's located at the back of Dom Funcjonalny, a 1928 villa designed by Czesław Przybylski.

❷ Lukullus

Many Varsovians' favourite pastry shop, **Lukullus** (https://cukiernia lukullus.pl; ul Walecznych 29; pastries 10-20zł; ⏱9am-9pm, to 8pm Sun) offers sweet and savoury treats, such as flaky croissants, traditional Polish poppy seed cake and cheesecake, that look and taste divine.

❸ Villa Przybytkowskich

A remarkable survivor from when Saska Kępa was a countryside village, **Villa Przybytkowskich** (ul Walecznych 37) is a two-storey wooden house that sits at an odd angle to the road layout and is still lived in by descendants of the family who occupied it in the 1880s.

❹ Agnieszka Osiecka Monument

This life-size, bronze **statue** (cnr ul Francuska & ul Obrońców) of an elegant woman sitting at a cafe table honours Agnieszka Osiecka (1936–97), a poet, journalist and writer of song lyrics. An icon of post-WWII Polish culture, Osiecka lived in Saska Kępa most of her life.

❺ Lachert Villa

Along ul Katowicka are several prime examples of modernist buildings, including this three-storey **villa** (ul Katowicka 9-11a) designed by Lachert and Szanajca using Le Corbusier's five points of modern architecture and completed in 1928.

❻ Cloudmine

South of ul Zwycięzców, ul Francuska changes name to ul Paryska – it's worth heading to the far south of the street to find **Cloudmine** (http://cloudmine.pl; ul Paryska 17; ⏱noon-8pm Mon-Fri, 11am-7pm Sat), a chic women's fashion and interior design boutique promoting the wares of local designers and artists.

❼ Biała

Designed in 1934 by Lucjan Korngold and Piotr Lubiński, this gorgeous modernist villa is nowadays home to **Biała** (www.facebook.com/bialazjediziwypij; ul Francuska 2; mains 26-38zł; ⏱8am-10pm Sun-Tue, to midnight Wed-Sat), a super-convivial all-day restaurant, cafe and bar that's as good for casual breakfast as it is for a leisurely dinner.

Worth A Trip 📭
Wilanów Palace & Park

Warsaw's top palace, commissioned by King Jan III Sobieski in 1677, has changed hands several times over the centuries, with each new owner adding a bit of baroque here and a touch of neoclassical there. Follow two routes around the magnificently restored palace to view gorgeous rooms packed with artistic baubles and treasures.

www.wilanow-palac.pl
adult/concession route 1, 20/15zł, route 2, 15/10zł, both routes 30/20zł

🕘 9.30am-6pm Sat-Mon & Wed, to 4pm Tue, Thu & Fri mid-Apr–mid-Oct, 9.30am-4pm Wed-Mon mid-Oct–mid-Apr

🚊 Wilanów

TRABANTOS/SHUTTERSTOCK ©

Inside the Palace

When King Jan III Sobieski decided this was the perfect spot for his country estate, there was already a village here called Milanów that had existed since the Middle Ages. The king renamed the village in Latin as 'Villa Nova', later Polonised into Wilanów (vee-*lah*-noof). Miraculously, Wilanów survived WWII almost unscathed, and most of its furnishings and art were retrieved and reinstalled after the war.

Until 2020 most of the palace's upper-floor rooms are closed for restoration, leaving two routes through the building to follow – we recommend you do both.

Route 1 includes the White Hall, the palace's largest room, hung with portraits of successive owners of Wilanów; the Garden Galleries decorated with beautiful 17th-century frescoes; the Royal Apartments of King Jan III; the neoclassical-style Grand Vestibule; and the **Potocki Museum**, named after Stanisław Kostka Potocki, owner of Wilanów from 1799 to 1821, who in 1805 opened his art collection to the general public.

Route 2 covers Princess Marshall Lubomirska's Apartments, an immaculately restored salon dating from the late 18th century and including the magnificent Chinese and Hunting Rooms. Also here is the **Storage Accessible for Visitors**, which allows a fascinating behind-the-scenes look at the restoration and care of the palace's collection of *objets d'art* and antiques.

Wilanów Park

Adjoining the palace is the splendid 45-hectare **park** (Park Wilanowski; ul Potockiego 10/16; adult/concession 5/3zł, Thu free; 🕓9am-8pm Apr, to 9pm May & Aug, to 10pm Jun & Jul, to 7pm Sep, to 4pm Oct-Mar; 🚌116 or 180), which contains a variety of landscaping. The central part comprises a manicured, two-level baroque Italian garden,

★ Top Tips

○ Book ahead for entry tickets (via phone or online) particularly on weekends and during the busy summer period.

○ Hire an audio guide (12zł) at the museum or download the free iiiGuide app to your smart phone before arriving.

○ Last entry to the palace is an hour before closing.

✖ Take a Break

Traditional Polish dishes are served in a superbly stylish communist-era interior at **Restauracja Wilanów** (📞22 842 1852; www.restauracja wilanow.com; ul Kostki Potockiego 27, Wilanów; mains 29-45zł; 🕓noon-10pm; 🚇Wilanów).

Enjoy a meal and live music and cabaret at **Kuźnia Kulturalna** (📞500 200 200; www.kuzniakulturalna. pl; ul Kostki Potockiego 24, Wilanów; 🕓11am-10pm; 🚇Wilanów).

which extends from the palace down to the lake; the south is Anglo-Chinese in design; the northern section is an English landscape park. There's also a Renaissance-inspired rose garden and the **Orangery** (☎ 22 544 2700; ul Potockiego 10/16; admission varies; ⏰ 9am-dusk Apr-Sep), which houses an art gallery displaying temporary exhibitions.

From the park you can view the palace's rear exterior, adorned with some murals, including a 17th-century sundial with a bas-relief of Chronos, god of time.

Poster Museum

Polish poster art is outstanding and can be enjoyed at the **Poster Museum** (Muzeum Plakatu; ☎ 22 842 2606; www.postermuseum.pl; ul Potock-iego 10/16; adult/concession 10/7zł, Mon free; ⏰ noon-4pm Mon, from 10am Tue-Sun), housed in a distinctive example of modernist architecture standing where the stables of Wilanów Palace were once located. The museum's collection numbers over 62,000 artistic, advertising and propaganda prints from around the world. Only a fraction of these are shown at any one time, but exhibitions change regularly. There's also a great selection of posters, postcards and books to buy.

St Anne's Church

Just outside the Wilanów Palace gates, the neo-rennaissance **St Anne's Church** (Kościół Rzymskokatolicki pw św Anny; ☎ 22 842 1801; http://parafiawilanow.pl;

Illuminations in the Golden Courtyard

Kolegiacka 1) dates from 1870, although there has been a church on this spot since the 14th century. The tombs of the Potocki and Branicki families, one-time owners of Wilanów Palace, are located here, as well as a giant mammoth bone, discovered on the site when the foundations of the building were being laid.

Temple of Divine Providence

For something completely different from Wilanów's royal flourishes, walk around 1km southwest of the palace to find the monumental **Temple of Divine Providence** (Świątynia Opatrznosci Bożej; ☎22 201 9712; www.centrumopatrznosci. pl; Błonia Wilanowskie; ⊙11am-8pm Mon-Sat, to 4pm Sun; ▣Świątynia Opatrzności Bożej). Opened in 2016, this Catholic church, with a dome

Royal Garden of Light

Come winter, Wilanów Palace and its park are transformed nightly by coloured illuminations into the **Royal Garden of Light** (Królewski Ogród Światła; admission 10zł; ⊙4-9pm Nov-Feb). On Saturday and Sunday, a 10-minute sound and light show including 3D holograms is projected across the palace facade at 6.30pm, 7.30pm and 8.30pm.

reminiscent of an enormous lemon squeezer, makes a bold contemporary statement. Its brutalist architecture may not be to everyone's taste, but the interior space supported by soaring ribbons of concrete is undeniably impressive.

DEJAN GOSPODAREK/SHUTTERSTOCK ©

Survival Guide

POLIN Museum of the History of Polish Jews (p86)
M.STAROWIEYSKA_D.GOLIK / POLIN MUSEUM OF THE HISTORY OF POLISH JEWS ©

Before You Go

Book Your Stay

Accommodation ranges from fun backpacker hostels to luxury boutique hotels, spread widely across the city centre; there are also plenty of centrally located rental apartments. Public transport is excellent so don't be afraid of staying slightly outside the centre to take advantage of lower accommodation rates. Note that many central hotels are geared towards business travellers and are priced accordingly (on a weekend many offer discounted rates).

Useful Websites

Don't neglect the internet; you have a good chance of snagging a bargain via online booking, rather than just fronting up to the reception desk.

Lonely Planet (lonelyplanet.com/poland/warsaw/hotels) Recommendations and

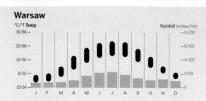

Warsaw

°C/°F Temp · Rainfall inches/mm

When to Go

○ **Spring & Summer**

May sees the city's parks and public spaces burst into greenery and flowers. Midsummer is wonderful for relaxing outside along the Vistula at bars, cafes and riverside beaches.

○ **Autumn & Winter**

In October cinema fans will enjoy the Warsaw Film Festival. There are Christmas markets from the end of November and outdoor ice rinks open from December through to March.

bookings.

Stay Poland (www.staypoland.com) Warsaw-based travel agency with an online accommodation booking service.

Best Budget

Dream Hostel (☏ 22 419 4848; https://dream-hostels.com; Krakowskie Przedmieście 55, Śródmieście Północne; dm/tw from 51/200zł; @ 🛜; 🚊 Plac Zamkowy) This lively hostel ticks all the right boxes and is close to the Old Town.

Chill Out Hostel (☏ 22 409 9881; www.chillout

hostel.pl; ul Poznańska 7/5, Śródmieście Południowe; d from 170zł, dm/s/d without bathroom from 43/129/156zł; 🚇 Plac Konstytucji) Stay in this colourfully decorated hostel with private rooms on trendy ul Poznańska.

Oki Doki City Hostel (☏ 22 828 0122; www.oki-doki.pl; Plac Dąbrowskiego 3, Śródmieście Północne; dm/d from 38/168zł; 🛜; Ⓜ Świętokrzyska) Justly popular hostel in a grand pre-WWII building, with a second branch in the New Town.

Best Midrange

Autor Rooms (📞 797 992 737; https://autor rooms.pl; ul Lwowska 17/7, Śródmieście Południowe; d from 434zł; 🛜; 🚇 Plac Konstytucji) Encounter contemporary Polish design at this cosy apartment close by top restaurants and bars.

Hotel Indigo Warsaw Nowy Świat (📞 22 418 8900; http://indigowar saw.com; ul Smolna 40, Śródmieście Północne; r from 415zł; ❄ @ 🛜; 🚇 Muzeum Narodowe) Dazzling design in the public areas and rooms at this super-classy business hotel.

Dom Literatury (📞 22 635 0404; https:// domliteratury.com.pl; ul Krakowskie Przedmieście 87/89, Stare Miasto; s/d 275/435zł; 🛜; 🚇 Stare Miasto) The lift (elevator) may be slow but the rooms are charming and right by the Old Town.

Best Top End

Hotel Bristol (📞 22 551 1000; www.hotelbristol warsaw.pl; ul Krakowskie Przedmieście 42/44, Śródmieście Północne; r from 665zł; ❄ 🛜 🏊; 🚇 Hotel Bristol) Historic

abode beloved by VIPs for its art nouveau interior design and luxe rooms.

Hotel Warszawa (📞 22 470 0300; https://wars zawa.hotel.com.pl; Plac Powstańców Warszawy 9, Śródmieście Północne; d from 800zł; ❄ @ 🛜 🏊; 🚇 Świętokrzyska) Superb makeover of a pre-WWII tower block into a designer's dream of a hotel.

H15 (📞 22 553 8700; www.h15boutiqueapart ments.com; ul Poznan-ska 15, Śródmieście Południowe; r/apt from 540/1250zł; 🅿 ❄ 🛜; 🚇 Hoża) Individually de-signed, luxury rooms in an elegant old building with excellent bars and restaurants close by.

Arriving in Warsaw

Warsaw Chopin Airport (Lotnisko Chopina Warszawy; 📞 22 650 4220; www.lotnisko-chopina.pl; ul Żwirki i Wigury 1, Włochy; 🚆 Warszawa Lotnisko Chopina) Warsaw's main airport, 9km south of the city centre, handles

most domestic and international flights.

Trains run to War-szawa Centralna (S3 Line) and Warszawa Śródmieście (S2 Line) train stations every 30 minutes to every hour, between 5am and 10.30pm (4.40zł, 20 minutes).

Bus 175 (4.40zł, every 15 minutes, 5am to 11pm) runs to the city, passing along ul Jerozolimiskie and ul Nowy Świat before terminating at Plac Piłsudskiego, within walking distance of the Old Town.

A taxi to the city should cost 35zł to 50zł, and the journey takes 20 to 30 minutes.

Buy tickets for public transport from newsagents at the airports.

Warsaw Modlin Airport (Modlin Lotnisko; 📞 22 315 1880; www.modlinairport. pl; ul Generała Wiktora Thommée 1a, Nowy Dwór Mazowiecki; 🚆 Modlin) Located 39km north of Warsaw, and is used by budget carriers, includ-ing Ryanair, for flights to and from the UK.

For train travel take the shuttle bus to nearby Modlin station, where you can catch a train to Warszawa Centralna (19zł for shuttle and train, one hour, at least hourly).

Modlin Bus (☑703 403 993; www.modlinbus. com; ticket 9-35zł) services run between the airport and the Palace of Culture & Science. Buy a ticket from the driver (35zł); advance fares bookable online are as low 9zł. The journey is around 55 minutes.

A taxi to the city centre costs 159zł between 6am and 10pm, and 199zł at night (30 to 40 minutes).

Warszawa Zachodnia bus terminal (Dworzec Autobusowy Warszawa Zachodnia; ☑22 823 6200, 24hr 703 403 403; www. dawz.pl; al Jerozolimskie 144, Czyste; ⊙information & tickets 5.30am-10pm) Handles the majority of international and domestic routes from the capital, run by various operators.

Warszawa Centralna (Warsaw Central; www. pkp.pl; al Jerozolimskie 54, Śródmieście Północne; ⊙24hr; 🚉Warszawa Centralna) Has direct trains to every major Polish city, several international cities and many other places in between; check the online timetable in English at http://roz-klad-pkp.pl for times and fares.

🚲 Getting Around

Bicycle

The Polish capital is mostly flat and easy to navigate, and cycle paths are on the increase. However, Warsaw drivers are fast and aggressive so you may end up following the locals' lead and sharing the footpath with pedestrians.

It's worth registering online (10zł) for the public bike-rental system **Veturilo** (www. veturilo.waw.pl). Available from March to November, it's free to use a bicycle for up to 20 minutes; 1zł for up to one hour, 3zł for up to two hours, 5zł for up to three hours and 7zł for up to four hours. Each additional hour thereafter is 2zł. Use the website to find pick-up and drop-off locations as well as where to find electric bikes.

Bus

Warsaw's extensive bus system is operated by **ZTM** (Zarząd Transportu Miejskiego; Municipal Transport Authority; ☑19 115; www.ztm.waw. pl) and uses the same ticketing system as the tram and metro lines.

You could also use the private hop-on, hop-off **City Sightseeing Warsaw** (☑793 795 733; www.warsaw.city-sight seeing.pl; 24/48/72hr tickets 60/80/90zł) service.

Buses operate from about 5am to midnight, and services are frequent and punctual, though often crowded during rush hours (7am to 9am and 3.30pm to 6.30pm Monday to Friday).

After midnight several night bus routes link major suburbs to the city centre.

Car & Motorcycle

● All the major international car-hire companies have offices

Tickets & Passes

Warsaw's tram, bus and metro lines all use the same ticketing system.

o For single journeys buy a 20-minute ticket (3.40zł). There are also 75- (4.40zł) and 90-minute (7zł) tickets; all allow transfers.

o If you will be using public transport a lot, consider a 24-hour ticket (zone one/one and two 15/26zł) or the three-day version (36/57zł).

o A weekend ticket (24zł for all zones) is valid from 7pm Friday to 8am Monday.

o Tickets valid for 30 and 90 days are also available but have to be bought from ZTM Passenger Service Points; see www.ztm.waw.pl for further details.

in Warsaw, many based at the airport. Polish companies offer cheaper rates, but may have fewer English-speaking staff and rental options.

o Most major hotels offer parking, although some charge handsomely for it – rates of 100zł are not uncommon.

o On the streets the entire city centre is a paid parking zone from 8am to 6pm Monday to Friday. Evenings, weekends and public holidays are free. Look for ticket machines on the streets where you will pay 3zł for the first hour, 3.60zł for the second hour, 4.20zł for the third hour

and 3zł for the fourth and subsequent hours. For full details see https://zdm.waw.pl.

o Warsaw's road rules are similar to much of the rest of Europe.

Metro

Warsaw's metro system, operated by ZTM, has two lines and uses the same ticketing system as the bus and tram lines.

o The north–south M1 line runs from the southern suburb of Ursynów (Kabaty station) to Młociny in the north via the city centre.

o The newer east–west line (M2) runs from

Rondo Daszyńskiego, west of the city centre, to Dworzec Wileński in Praga; there are future plans to extend this line.

o The lines intersect at Świętokrzyska station.

o Yellow signs with a big red letter 'M' indicate the entrances to metro stations.

o Every metro station has a public toilet.

o There are lifts for passengers with disabilities.

o Metro lines run from about 5am to midnight, and services are frequent and punctual, running approximately every eight minutes and every four minutes during rush hour (7am to 9am and 3.30pm to 6.30pm Monday to Friday) when carriages can be crowded.

o On Friday and Saturday nights the metro runs until around 3am.

Taxi

o Taxis in Warsaw are easily available and not too expensive, costing 8zł flag fall and around 2/4zł per kilometre during the day/night within the city centre. A typical 10-minute ride should cost around 20zł.

○ All official taxis in Warsaw have their meters adjusted to the appropriate tariff, so you just pay whatever the meter displays. When you board a taxi, make sure the meter is turned on in your presence, which ensures you don't have the previous passenger's fare added to yours.

○ Taxis can be waved down on the street, but it's preferable to order a taxi by phone.

○ Apps such as Taxify and Uber are highly popular ways of booking taxis.

Tram

Warsaw's trams are operated by ZTM and use the same ticketing system as the bus and metro lines.

Lines run from about 5am to midnight, and services are frequent and punctual, though often crowded during rush hours (7am to 9am and 3.30pm to 6.30pm Monday to Friday).

Train

Warsaw's suburban trains are run by Koleje Mazowieckie (www.mazowieckie.com.

pl), SKM (www.skm.warszawa.pl) and WKD (http://wkd.com.pl). They are useful for connecting with the airports, crossing between either side of the Vistula or heading out to Warsaw's far-flung suburbs.

As long as you stay within the zones covered by ZTM, you can also use the integrated bus/metro/tram tickets on suburban trains, including the service to Warsaw Chopin Airport.

Many suburban services pass through or originate from Warszawa Śródmieście, which is between Warszawa Centralna train station and Centrum metro station.

Essential Information

Accessible Travel

Cobblestones and stairs present challenging mobility issues in Warsaw's Old Town, and many older buildings, including hotels

and museums, are not wheelchair friendly. However, all new buildings, including modern museums, art galleries, shopping malls and train stations, are designed to be accessible, and an increasing number of older buildings are being retrofitted with ramps, lifts and wider doors.

In terms of public transport, most trains, buses and trams have ramps and are designed to accommodate wheelchairs.

Download Lonely Planet's free Accessible Travel guides from http://lptravel.to/AccessibleTravel.

Business Hours

Most places open the following hours. Shopping centres generally open longer hours and from 9am to 8pm at weekends. Museums usually close Mondays, and may have shorter hours from December to March.

Banks 8am–6pm Monday to Friday, to 1pm Saturday (varies)

Offices 9am–5pm

Monday to Friday, to 1pm Saturday (varies)

Post Offices Main office 24 hours, other branches 8am–7pm Monday to Friday, to 1pm Saturday

Restaurants 11am–10pm

Shops 8am–6pm Monday to Saturday

Shopping Malls 10am–10pm

Discount Cards

Available from all Warsaw tourist offices, the **Warsaw Pass** (www.warsawpass.com) card costs 129/169/199zł for 24/48/72 hours, and covers admission to 17 of the city's major attractions, including the Chopin Museum, Royal Łazienki Museum and the PKiN observation deck, as well as unlimited travel on the hop-on, hop-off bus run by **City Sightseeing Warsaw** (📞 793 795 733; www.warsaw.city-sightseeing.pl; 24/48/72hr tickets 60/80/90zł).

Electricity

Type C
220V/50Hz

Type E
220V/50Hz

Money

ATMs and *kantors* (currency-exchange kiosks) are fairly common. Credit cards are generally accepted and often preferred to cash.

Banks

Bank Pekao (www.pekao.com.pl; Plac Bankowy 2, Śródmieście Północne; Ⓜ Ratusz Arsenał) has several branches in the city centre; other locations include the **Marriott Hotel** (al Jerozolimskie 65/79, Śródmieście Południowe; 🕐 8am-7pm Mon-Fri; Ⓡ Warszawa Centralna) and **Plac Bankowy** (ul Krakowskie Przedmieście 1, Śródmieście Północne; Ⓜ Nowy Świat-Uniwersytet).

Changing Money

There are 24-hour *kantors* at **Warszawa Centralna** (p145) train station and at **Warsaw Chopin Airport** (p146). Beware of *kantors* that are open late at night as they tend to offer poor rates.

Exchange Rates

Australia	A$1	2.7zł
Canada	C$1	2.9zł
Europe	€1	4.3zł
Japan	¥100	3.4zł
New Zealand	NZ$1	2.6zł
UK	£1	5.0zł
USA	US$1	3.8zł

For current exchange rates, see www.xe.com.

Tipping

Tipping is customary in restaurants, cafes and at service establishments such as hairdressers; optional elsewhere.

Hotels Not expected but can leave 10zł per night for housekeeper; similar for porters and helpful concierges.

Restaurants Standard is 10%. At smaller establishments and for smaller tabs round to nearest 5zł or 10zł increment. Leave tip in cash if you pay bill by credit card.

Taxis Round up the fare for good service.

Public Holidays

New Year's Day 1 January

Epiphany 6 January

Easter Sunday March or April

Easter Monday March or April

Labour Day 1 May

Constitution Day 3 May

Pentecost Sunday Seventh Sunday after Easter

Corpus Christi Ninth Thursday after Easter

Assumption Day 15 August

All Saints' Day 1 November

Independence Day 11 November

Christmas 25 and 26 December

Safe Travel

○ Overall Warsaw is a safe place to visit, but you should take precautions while walking at night.

○ Watch your possessions on public transport and in other crowded places.

○ Bikes are particularly at risk; try not to leave your bike out of sight for too long, and always lock it firmly with the strongest lock you can find.

Telephone

All telephone numbers, landline and mobile, have nine digits. There are no city or area codes.

To call abroad from Poland, dial the international access code (✆00), then the country code, then the area code (minus any initial zero) and the number. To dial Poland from abroad, dial your country's international access code, then ✆48 (Poland's country code) and then the unique nine-digit local number.

Mobile Phones

Poland uses the GSM 900/1800 system, the same as Europe, Australia and New Zealand. It's not compatible with some phones from North America or Japan; check with your service provider.

If your mobile phone is unlocked, a cheaper and often better option is to buy a prepaid local SIM card, available from any mobile-phone shop. Prepaid SIMs allow you to make local calls at cheaper local rates. In this case, of course, you can't use your existing mobile number.

There's also the option of using an internet phone service such as Skype.

Toilets

○ Toilets are labelled 'toaleta' or 'WC'.

○ Men should look for

Dos & Don'ts

Greetings It's customary to greet people, including shopkeepers, on entering with a friendly *'dzień dobry'* (jyen do·bri; good day). On leaving, part with a hearty *'do widzenia'* (do vee·dze·nya; goodbye).

Religion Treat churches and monasteries with respect and keep conversation to a minimum. It's always best to wear proper attire, including trousers for men and covered shoulders and longer skirts (no short shorts) for women. Refrain from flash photography and remember to leave a small donation in the box by the door. If visiting a synagogue or a Jewish cemetery, men should cover their heads with a hat or cap.

Eating & Drinking When raising a glass, greet your Polish friends with *'na zdrowie'* (nah zdroh·vee·ya; cheers)! Before tucking into your food, wish everyone *'smacznegos'* (smach·neh·go; bon appetit)! End the meal by saying *'dziękuję'* (jyen·koo·ye; thank you).

'dla panów' or *'męski',* or a door marked by a downward-pointing triangle.

o Women should head for *'dla pań'* or *'damski',* or a door marked with a circle.

o Public toilets often charge a fee of 2zł, collected by a toilet attendant sitting at the door. Have small change ready.

Tourist Information

Tourist Office – PKiN (www.warsawtour.pl; Plac Defilad 1, Śródmieście Północne; ☺8am-7pm May-Sep, to 6pm Oct-Apr; ☎; Ⓜ Centrum, ⓇWarszawa Śródmieście) Warsaw's official tourist information organisation provides maps, leaflets and plenty of friendly advice. There's no phone number, so visit in person.

Tourist Office – Old Town (Rynek Starego Miasta 19/21, Stare Miasto; ☺9am-8pm May-Sep, to 6pm Oct-Apr; ☎; Ⓡ Stare Miasto)

Tourist Office – Praga (Plac Koneser, Szmulow-izna; ☺11am-7pm)

Visas

EU citizens do not need visas and can stay indefinitely. Citizens of the USA, Canada, Australia, New Zealand, Israel, Japan and many other countries can stay in Poland for up to 90 days without a visa.

Other nationalities should check with their local Polish embassy or on the Polish Ministry of Foreign Affairs website (www.gov.pl/web/diplomacy).

Survival Guide Essential Information

Language

Poland is linguistically one of the most homogeneous countries in Europe – more than 95% of the population has Polish as their first language. Polish belongs to the Slavic language family, with Czech and Slovak as close relatives. It has about 45 million speakers.

Vowels are generally pronounced short, giving them a 'clipped' quality. Note that **a** is pronounced as the 'u' in 'cut', **ai** as in 'aisle' and **ow** as in 'cow'. If you read the pronunciation guides in this chapter as if they were English you'll be understood just fine. Note that stressed syllables are indicated with italics.

To enhance your trip with a phrasebook, visit **lonelyplanet.com**.

Basics

Hello.
Cześć.   cheshch

Goodbye.
Do widzenia.   do vee·*dze*·nya

Yes./No.
Tak./Nie.   tak/nye

Please./You're welcome.
Proszę.   *pro*·she

Thank you.
Dziękuję.   jyen·*koo*·ye

Excuse me./Sorry.
Przepraszam.   pshe·*pra*·sham

How are you?
Jak pan/pani   yak pan/*pa*·nee
się miewa? (m/f)   shye *mye*·va

Fine. And you?
Dobrze.   *dob*·zhe
A pan/pani? (m/f)   a pan/*pa*·nee

Do you speak English?
Czy pan/pani   chi pan/*pa*·nee
mówi po   *moo*·vee po
angielsku? (m/f)   po an·*gyel*·skoo

I don't understand.
Nie rozumiem.   nye ro·*zoo*·myem

Eating & Drinking

I'd like the menu, please.
Proszę o   *pro*·she o
jadłospis.   ya·*dwo*·spees

I don't eat meat
Nie jadam   nye ya·dam
mięsa   *myen*·sa

Cheers!
Na zdrowie!   na *zdro*·vye

Please bring the bill.
Proszę o   *pro*·she o
rachunek.   ra·*khoo*·nek

Shopping

I'd like to buy ...
Chcę kupić ...   khtse *koo*·peech

I'm just looking.
Tylko oglądam.   *til*·ko o·*glon*·dam

How much is it?
Ile to kosztuje?   *ee*·le to kosh·*too*·ye

That's too expensive.
To jest za drogie. to yest za dro·gye

Can you lower the price?
Czy może pan/ chi mo·zhe pan/
pani obniżyć pa·nee ob·nee·zhich
cenę? (m/f) tse·ne

Emergencies

Help!
Na pomoc! na po·mots

Go away!
Odejdź! o·deyj

Call the police!
Zadzwoń po zad·zvon' po
policję! po·lee·tsye

Call a doctor!
Zadzwoń po zad·zvon' po
lekarza! le·ka·zha

I'm lost.
Zgubiłem/ zgoo·bee·wem/
am się. (m/f) wam shye

I'm ill.
Jestem yes·tem
chory/a. (m/f) kho·ri/ra

Where are the toilets?
Gdzie są toalety? gjye som to·a·le·ti

Time & Numbers

What time is it?
Która jest ktoo·ra yest
godzina? go·jee·na

It's one o'clock.
Pierwsza. pyerf·sha

Half past (10).
Wpół do fpoow do
(jedenastej). (ye·de·nas·tey)

morning
rano ra·no

afternoon
popołudnie po·po·wood·nye

evening
wieczór vye·choor

yesterday
wczoraj fcho·rai

today
dziś/dzisiaj jeesh/jee·shai

tomorrow
jutro yoo·tro

1	jeden	ye·den
2	dwa	dva
3	trzy	tshi
4	cztery	chte·ri
5	pięć	pyench
6	sześć	sheshch
7	siedem	shye·dem
8	osiem	o·shyem
9	dziewięć	jye·vyench
10	dziesięć	jye·shench

Transport & Directions

Where's a/the ...?
Gdzie jest ...? gjye yest ...

What's the address?
Jaki jest adres? ya·kee yest ad·res

Can you show me (on the map)?
Czy może pan/ chi mo·zhe pan/
pani mi pa·nee mee
pokazać po·ka·zach
(na mapie)? (m/f) (na ma·pye)

When's the next (bus)?
Kiedy jest kye·di yest
następny nas·temp·ni
(autobus)? (ow·to·boos)

A ... ticket (to Katowice).
Proszę bilet pro·she bee·let
... (do Katowic). ... (do ka·to·veets)

Behind the Scenes

Send Us Your Feedback

We love to hear from travellers – your comments help make our books better. We read every word, and we guarantee that your feedback goes straight to the authors. Visit **lonelyplanet.com/contact** to submit your updates and suggestions.

Note: We may edit, reproduce and incorporate your comments in Lonely Planet products such as guidebooks, websites and digital products, so let us know if you don't want your comments reproduced or your name acknowledged. For a copy of our privacy policy visit lonelyplanet.com/privacy.

Simon's Thanks

A particular thanks to locals Konrad Pyzel, Noam Silberberg and Micheal Moran; and to Sarah Johnstone for keeping me company. In memory of members of my family and my dear departed friend Dora Grynberg, all of whom had the good fortune to escape – and to the many, many others who sadly did not and whose ghosts will forever haunt Warsaw.

Acknowledgements

Cover photograph: Sigismund's Column (p43), Old Town, Karol Kozlowski/AWL Images©

Photographs pp30–31 (left to right): Antonistock/getty images; Juliusz Klosowski/Shutterstock © architect Rainer Mahlamäki; Michal Bednarek/500px ©.

This Book

This 1st edition of Lonely Planet's *Pocket Warsaw* guidebook was researched and written by Simon Richmond. This guidebook was produced by the following:

Destination Editor
Gemma Graham

Senior Product Editors
Sandie Kestell,

Genna Patterson

Regional Senior Cartographer Valentina Kremenchutskaya

Product Editor Shona Gray

Book Designer
Virginia Moreno

Assisting Book Designer
Wibowo Rusli

Assisting Editors
Andrew Bain, Judith

Bamber, Nigel Chin, Samantha Forge, Carly Hall, Gabrielle Innes, Kellie Langdon, Anne Mulvaney, Rosie Nicholson, Lauren O'Connell, Kristin Odijk, Tamara Sheward, Gabrielle Stefanos

Cover Researcher
Naomi Parker

Thanks to Imogen Bannister, Kate James

Index

See also separate subindexes for:

⊗ Eating p157
🍷 Drinking p158
☆ Entertainment p159
🔒 Shopping p159

Sights 000
Map Pages 000

Our Writers

Simon Richmond

Journalist and photographer Simon Richmond first worked for Lonely Planet in 1999 on their Central Asia guide. He's since researched and written guidebooks to many countries, including Australia, China, Greece, India, Indonesia, Iran, Japan, Malaysia, Mongolia, Myanmar (Burma), Russia, Singapore, South Africa, South Korea,Turkey and the USA. He's penned features for Lonely Planet's website on topics from the world's best swimming pools to the joys of Urban Sketching – follow him on Instagram (@simonrichmond) to see some of his photos and sketches. His travel features have been published in many publications, including in the UK's *Independent*, *Guardian*, *Times* and *Daily Telegraph* newspapers, and the *Royal Geographical Society Magazine*; and Australia's *Sydney Morning Herald* and *Australian* newspapers, and *Australian Financial Review Magazine*.

Published by Lonely Planet Global Limited
CRN 554153
1st edition – Feb 2020
ISBN 978 1 78 868 467 5
© Lonely Planet 2020   Photographs © as indicated 2020
10 9 8 7 6 5 4 3 2 1
Printed in Singapore

All rights reserved. No part of this publication may be copied, stored in a retrieval system, or transmitted in any form by any means, electronic, mechanical, recording or otherwise, except brief extracts for the purpose of review, and no part of this publication may be sold or hired, without the written permission of the publisher. Lonely Planet and the Lonely Planet logo are trademarks of Lonely Planet and are registered in the US Patent and Trademark Office and in other countries. Lonely Planet does not allow its name or logo to be appropriated by commercial establishments, such as retailers, restaurants or hotels. Please let us know of any misuses: lonelyplanet.com/ip.